COOKBOOK THE HEIRLOOM TOMATO

THE

HEIRLOOM TOMATO

COOKBOOK

TEXT BY MIMI LUEBBERMANN

PHOTOGRAPHS BY DAN MILLS AND ROBERT HOLMES

CHRONICLE BOOKS

SAN FRANCISCO

Recipe page 60, reprinted with the permission of the author from
    Jimtown Store Cookbook: Recipes from Sonoma County's Favorite Country
    Market; HarperCollins Publishers, 2002
Recipe pages 89–90, adapted from Polenta, by Brigit Legere Binns,
    Chronicle Books, 1997
Recipes pages 51, 56, 66, 72, and 81, adapted from The Little Red Tomato
    Primer © 2004 by Lark Creek Restaurant Group

Library of Congress Cataloging-in-Publication Data available.

ISBN-10: 0-8118-5355-1
ISBN-13: 978-0-8118-5355-2

Manufactured in China

Packaged and designed by Jennifer Barry Design, Fairfax, CA
Layout production by Kristen Wurz
Recipe testing by Catherine Pantsios
Prop styling by Diane McGauley
Food styling by Stephanie Greenleigh
Copyedited by Carolyn Miller

Distributed in Canada by Raincoast Books
9050 Shaughnessy Street
Vancouver, British Columbia V6P 6E5

10 9 8 7 6 5 4 3 2

Chronicle Books LLC
680 Second Street
San Francisco, California 94107

www.chroniclebooks.com

CONTENTS

INTRODUCTION

What on earth has happened to tomatoes? Sneaking in among the tennis-ball-size, almost red, tasteless tomatoes are the new stars. When most of us were not looking, heirloom tomatoes were creeping up on us. The tomatoes we recognized in our grocery stores have run off to costume themselves in red, yellow, and pink blotches; to dance in green zebra stripes; and to deck themselves out in deep, corrugated furls of brick red. And don't forget about the dusky rose-blushed blacks, the tangerine oranges, the light whites, and the bright sunlight yellows.

Welcome to the world of the heirloom tomato, which has turned the mundane commercial tomato into a has-been. Brilliantly colored tomatoes are making a splash in home-grown gardens, farmers' markets, and farm stands all over America. Aside from their showy colors and weird shapes, they taste just like tomatoes should taste in the full ripeness of summer: delicious! Chefs vie to produce platters of cherry tomatoes dazzling in rainbow colors of green, red, rusty-brown, orange, and pink. European-style salads pair farmstead cheeses with tomatoes, and of course, pungent basil imbues its fragrance to deep-flavored heirloom tomatoes in drinks like Bloody Marys and dishes like cinnamon-basil ice cream or tomato marmalade. It is a tasty revolution.

In truth, this tomato paradise has been a while in coming. For several decades, tomato lovers were limited to commercial tomato hybrids with little taste, no perfume, and the texture of India rubber. Then, American travelers to Europe in the 1980s tasted lovely farm tomatoes and were so delighted by the experience that once home, they rejected run-of-the-mill American supermarket tomatoes. Chefs began to search out farmers to grow flavorful European varieties for them, and suddenly, the great heirloom chase was on. Chefs, farmers, and small culinary seed catalogues discovered that not everyone had jumped on the hybrid tomato bandwagon. Hidden-away home gardeners had passed on their favorite tomato seeds from family to family, neighbor to neighbor. Regional seed catalogues and little-known seed banks were hoarding varieties that had been around for decades, even centuries. Digging deep, we discovered that we had our own old-fashioned, great-tasting tomatoes here in America.

You might ask, "What is an heirloom tomato, anyway?" and to be sure, the answer is not as easy as eating a sun-warmed tomato right off the vine. Botanically, the tomato is named *Lycopersicon esculentum,* and it is a member of the Solanaceae family, which includes eggplants, peppers, potatoes, and tomatillos among its edible members. Gardeners have always experimented, cross-breeding their plants, stroking pollen from one plant's flower onto the flower of another and then eagerly waiting to see the results over the next few years. However, plant breeders have manipulated the genes of tomatoes by selective breeding, not for taste or color but for disease resistance. In their haste to make a commercial tomato that could withstand soil-borne diseases and different pests, the breeders forgot about the texture and flavor of the tomato.

Strolling down the vegetable aisles of a plant nursery, you can see vast numbers of hybridized tomatoes, which promise much disease resistance but often result in a fruit with such an insipid flavor that salt, pepper, and even extra-virgin olive oil cannot improve it. Not so with heirloom tomatoes, which celebrate good taste. An heirloom tomato differs from a hybrid in that it is open-pollinated; that is, the flower is pollinated with pollen from another plant to make a fruit with seeds that can reproduce the tomato. The seeds of hybrid tomatoes are viable, but they do not reproduce themselves as do the open-pollinated types. Most seed catalogues define heirlooms as varieties documented to be fifty years old, while others are more liberal with their standards. Everyone agrees that heirlooms were bred for flavor and that they taste rich and sweet, with a fine acid balance. They are the essence of summer.

You will find a good deal of dissent on which heirloom tomato is the very best. Preference is based on each person's palate. Some have a predilection for sweet tomatoes, like the yellows and oranges with little acid ping, while others lean toward a tomato with a more obvious balance of tartness and sweetness. Growing conditions add their own say-so to the competition, as a warmer microclimate will develop more sugar in the fruit in one location, while a block away, a windier garden might produce a less-sweet tomato of the same variety. Everyone's list of favorites will be different.

Many of the heirlooms come with wonderful stories attached, histories that add to the delight of growing them. You usually can spot an heirloom by its name: Black From Tula, Aunt Ruby's German Green, Georgia Streak, or Blondkopfchen. Mortgage Lifter, an old-time variety widely available, tells the tale of a gardener who recognized the worth of a tomato he found growing among his plants, carefully saved the seeds, and then was able to pay off his mortgage from the proceeds of his harvest from that plant over the next several years.

● ● ● The History of the Tomato

The tomato has a long history, beginning with wild vines growing in the coastal highlands of South America, from Chile to Peru. From there, the fruit traveled, perhaps propagated by birds, north to Central America. It was noted for the first time in history when Cortez and his retinue encountered it during his conquest of Mexico in 1519. The tomato, along with chocolate and corn, was among the strange foods Europeans found being served as part of the celebrated feasts of the Aztecs. The Spaniards, globe-trotting imperialists, sent tomato seeds to all their colonies, spreading its culinary fame throughout the Far East and, of course, back to Spain and from there to Italy, then under Spanish domination.

In the early days of their cultivation in America, tomatoes were grown for ornamental display only, as popular opinion held that the fruits were lethal to eat. This reputation was a hand-me-down from the earliest written texts, when the tomato's reputation was tainted by its association with certain deadly members of their plant family. The Solanaceae family, also known as the nightshade family, may claim petunias, peppers, eggplant, and potatoes as kissing kin, but the family also includes the deadly nightshade. There are many tales, hotly disputed as either fact or legend, about various sponsors who ate large quantities of tomatoes in public, surrounded by crowds who hoped to see the victims writhe in an agony of being poisoned by the dreadful fruit. The belief that tomatoes were poisonous died slowly, until by the 1820s tomatoes found their way into the earliest American cookbooks, at last on their way to becoming a staple of American cuisine.

The story of the introduction of the tomato to America is more tangled, with some historians claiming that the Spanish brought the tomato to their American colonies before they retroceded them to France. According to the limited documentation that exists, the growing and eating of tomatoes went from south to north. Thomas Jefferson, renowned as a gardener always willing to try something new, is believed to have grown seeds given to him by a Spanish neighbor.

One vexing question waits to be answered. Is the tomato a fruit or a vegetable? In botanical terms, the tomato is a fruit, the developed ovary of a seed plant. In the political arena, however, its true nature has been the subject of great debate. In 1863, the U.S. Supreme Court defined it as a vegetable in the case of *Nix* v. *Hedden*, because, as the winning argument ran, it was served with vegetables during the main course of the meal, never as dessert. The case came about because Congress had passed a Tariff Act to tax imported vegetables, and tomatoes were a huge imported crop, coming in from warmer climes before American farmers could harvest theirs in summer. If they were considered a fruit, they would have fallen outside the purview of the act.

Tomatoes entered the political arena again in 1980s during the Reagan administration, when ketchup was defined as a vegetable so that school lunch programs could fulfill federal guidelines more inexpensively. Yet whether they are fruit or vegetable hardly matters in the final analysis, as long as they are heirloom, sun-ripened, and available.

● ● ● The Heirloom Tomato Gardens and Festival at the Kendall-Jackson Wine Center

The gardens of the Kendall-Jackson Wine Center are located in Santa Rosa, California. Luther Burbank, the twentieth-century plant hybridizer and propagator, would have approved the location, not far from his own garden, which he called "the chosen spot of all this earth" for its superior combination of soil and climate. In the Vegetable Trial Gardens, the Wine Center's garden team grows over 180 varieties of heirloom tomatoes, a dozen different basils, and herbs and vegetables from all over the world.

The Heirloom Tomato Festival started after noted garden authority Jeff Dawson, now garden curator of the food and wine center Copia, in Napa, California, became head gardener. Working in a large winery garden to the north, he had fallen sway to the lure of heirloom tomatoes, planting large tracts of them there and instituting a seed collection. When he moved to the Kendall-Jackson gardens, he brought his enthusiasm with him. The first festival, in 1997, was a small, informal celebration of the initial harvest of heirlooms, with about three hundred attendees. A decade later, the festival has grown into a major event, with over twenty-five hundred people attending and myriad events during the tomato-packed day.

The Kendall-Jackson festival follows in a long line of events celebrating the tomato. There are tomato festivals in Europe, South America, and throughout America, although one of the most famous in Spain is really a tomato battle, with tomatoes hurled at contestants until the streets are ankle deep in tomato purée.

Like other enthusiasts, the Kendall-Jackson chefs were bowled over by the beauty and flavor of the heirlooms and couldn't wait to come up with recipes that matched the deliciousness of the tomatoes with the sun-kissed flavors of Kendall-Jackson wines. The success of these recipes sparked the idea of inviting chefs from some of the best Bay Area restaurants to participate in an expanded Heirloom Tomato Festival.

Patricia Rossi, the current garden director at Kendall-Jackson, supervises the planting and growing of every tomato in the garden. They are set out in ranks according to color, and the seeds are carefully saved after each harvest for next year's planting. Some seeds are available for sale during the festival and for several months afterward in the Wine Center. Currently, there are over twelve hundred heirloom tomato varieties in the Kendall-Jackson seed collection. Rossi rotates the locations of the

tomatoes yearly to minimize soil-borne diseases in the organic garden. She admits that she too has fallen for heirlooms. "I love them," she says, shaking her head. Not only does she spend her time caring for them, she spreads the gospel through phone conversations, answering questions on varieties and sharing cultivation tips with customers who have bought seeds, either at the festival or from the Wine Center. Calls also come in from all over America and even internationally about the ways and rules of starting tomato festivals, and Rossi often finds herself providing some special heirloom tomatoes for display in other celebrations of the fruit.

In September, when the northern California tomato harvest is at its peak, the spacious lawn behind the Kendall-Jackson Wine Center becomes the site of the festival. A community event, the festival benefits the School Garden Network of Sonoma County. Earlier in the week, the garden-inspired art contest and exhibition, which has both adult and youth categories, has contributors streaming into the exhibition hall carrying large cases and framed works. On the Thursday before festival day, the festival staff logs in tomatoes from a long line of home growers for the heirloom tomato taste-off contest, with expert judges weighing the merits of the submitted tomatoes by look, taste, and weight. The judges, after sampling each delectable tomato, award ribbons for the Heaviest, Biggest, and Best of Show for Quality, as well as the Best Red, Yellow/Orange, Paste, and Cherry Tomato, and one category of All Other Colors.

Early on the morning of the event, the staff sets up the tasting tables, slicing and dicing the 160 or so varieties grown in the Vegetable Trial Garden selected for the tasting. Displayed on white china plates and carefully labeled, the samples provide a rare opportunity for tomato novices and cognoscenti alike to sample a wide variety of heirloom tomatoes, which of course, fires the ambition of serious gardeners to grow some just like them the next year. The table selling seeds is busy.

By midmorning, grills along Bruschetta Boulevard are glowing, ready to start the California-style version of that famed Italian dish. There, festival-goers have the opportunity to taste different tomatoes prepared in a variety of bruschetta recipes that are carefully paired with Kendall-Jackson wines, from Chardonnay and Sauvignon Blanc to Pinot Noir and Cabernet Sauvignon. The booths for chefs from Bay Area restaurants line both sides of the

lawn. Stationed underneath the walnut trees for shade from the Indian summer sun, the chefs serve up dishes using regional ingredients to create memorable tomato dishes: Southwestern Heirloom Tomato Salad, Cherokee Purple Tomato BLT Sandwich, and Baked Stuffed Heirloom Tomatoes with Lobster Sauce are just some of the delicious assortment of dishes set out for attendees. The recipes in this book are testimonials to the creativity of chefs when presented with such exciting ingredients as heirloom tomatoes.

At 11 A.M., the guests begin to stream in. The food-and-wine-pairing seminars beckon. Along with the art exhibition, there are talks on growing heirloom tomatoes given by a local master gardener and live entertainment by local musicians. The crowning touch of the afternoon is the Chefs' Challenge contest, with four chefs set up behind a bank of stoves, each station backed by a refrigerator stocked with the same assortment of ingredients for each chef. In the front and center of each cooking stage is a large basket filled with a miscellany of tomatoes: plums, pastes, cherries, big beefs, and slicers. The chefs go to work, deftly creating masterpieces from the unexpected ingredients in their refrigerators and the extravagant sample of tomatoes in the baskets. After the allotted time is up, their dishes are judged and the grand award is presented. The cheering crowd is always dazzled by the results.

The Kendall-Jackson festival is unusual in its educational slant. It's true that superb wines, exquisite tomatoes, and the skills of fine chefs result in a delightful and delicious experience. Yet in a deeper sense, the festival strives to preserve and protect an agricultural heritage that almost slipped away. As a nation, we almost settled for insipid, uninspired, convenient produce, as easy to ship as a Granny Smith apple but unrewarding in taste and appearance. At Kendall-Jackson, the festival-goers' lively debate on the taste, color, perfume, and texture of the tomatoes as they stroll from table to table underscores a reemergence of the heritage of old tomato varieties. Many of them were carefully cultivated by our ancestors and grown from seeds that may have entered this country in the hem of a dress as a way to remember the land the immigrants left behind. Those tables, laden with decades and centuries of gardeners' careful work, from the planting to the saving of the seeds from year to year, allow us to remember our heritage and to protect our future.

● ● ● Twenty Favorite Heirloom Tomato Varieties

Kendall-Jackson garden director Patricia Rossi likes to think of this as a starter list, meant to change from year to year. All her tomatoes are beloved, but the ones in this list are some of the very best heirloom varieties as judged by color, shape, and taste. You will note that many of these same varieties were chosen by the participating chefs to be featured in their recipes. It's a great list, but there are hundreds more to try.

When selecting tomatoes to grow yourself, keep in mind that most heirloom varieties are indeterminate, meaning that they continue to grow and fruit all season long. Determinate varieties bear fruit all at once, so you will need to stagger the planting of those varieties to prolong their availability throughout the season.

Aunt Ruby's German Green: A beefsteak variety dressed in green, with yellow and pink blushes. The sweet flavor is balanced with spicy overtones. The smooth fruit weighs in at about 1 pound. Indeterminate; 80 days.

Big White Pink Stripe: Pale-peach-colored fruits with a pinkish blush on the blossom end and a peach-cream flesh. The 4-inch-diameter tomatoes with hints of melon have a nice acid balance to their sweet taste. Indeterminate; 95 days.

Black Brandywine: The same rich winey flavor as a Pink Brandywine, but with the undertones of the black varieties. Brandywines often excel in taste tests as the best of the best, so this one is worth raising. A flattened beefsteak in shape, it ranges from 8 to 12 ounces. Indeterminate; 80 days.

Black From Tula: A Russian beefsteak tomato with reddish brown shoulders, this fruit weighs in at 8 to 12 ounces. The vine sets flowers even when the weather is hot. The deep, rich, purple tomato flavor is nicely balanced with just a hint of acid. Indeterminate; 75 to 80 days.

Blondkopfchen: The German name translates to "little blonde girl." This variety produces abundant clusters of 20 to 30 delicious golden grape-size cherry tomatoes. Indeterminate; 75 days.

Brandywine OTV: Big red tomatoes borne on a potato-leafed plant with a yield greater than most of its more fickle Brandywine relatives. A cross between a Yellow Brandywine and an unknown red tomato, its initials OTV stand for "Off the Vine," an heirloom-tomato newsletter formerly published by Carolyn Male and Craig Le Houllier. The fruit harvests at about 1 pound, with well-balanced acids and sugars. Like all Brandywines, this one packs a full, deep, satisfying tomato taste. Indeterminate; 85 days.

Cherokee Purple: Attributed to the Cherokee tribe, the 10- to 12-ounce fruit glows a rosy brownish purple with a deep brick-red flesh. It has a thin skin and a soft flesh, and the taste is delicious, with the perfect sweet and rich flavor of a real tomato. The Cherokee needs to be picked ripe and eaten quickly, as it is quite perishable. Indeterminate; 80 days.

Emerald Evergreen: A beefsteak variety that is green when ripe. Mild in flavor, with little acid, and medium to large in size (10 to 12 ounces), it is a low-acid, all-purpose slicer for hamburgers and salads. Indeterminate; 72 days.

Eva's Purple Ball: One of the nineteenth-century heirlooms, the Eva's hails from the Black Forest region of Germany. The plants will stand up to hot, humid climates, and the dark purple fruits with a pinkish cast are perfect for salads and sandwiches, ranging from 4 to 5 ounces in size. The flavor has rich and full tones when harvested ripe. Indeterminate; 70 days.

Flammé: Those French farmers know their tomatoes, and this persimmon-orange salad heirloom, also known as Jaune Flammé, is stunning on both the vine and the plate. The 2- to 3-ounce tomatoes are rich in sweet flavor, with a firm texture and a fruity perfume. Extremely productive. Indeterminate; 65 to 70 days.

Georgia Streak: A big beautiful beefsteak from Georgia, the predominantly yellow flesh has streaks of bright carmine throughout. The flavor is sprightly, with a lightly acid but very sweet taste. Expect 2-pounders early in the season, with lots of 1-pounders through the summer. Indeterminate; 85 to 90 days.

Green Grape: The size and color of a green grape, but packed with zesty tang and a sweet flavor. The plants are determinate and consequently compact, but constant picking will extend the harvest season. A wonderful small cherry tomato for salads or for dipping. Determinate; 70 to 85 days.

Green Zebra: A 2-inch-diameter salad tomato that packs a punch both in its surprising yellowy green exterior with dark green stripes and its bright green interior, and its sweet-tart flavor with lemon overtones. Indeterminate; 75 to 80 days.

Mirabell: A loose-limbed, rangy plant that produces tiny, less-than-$\frac{1}{2}$-inch-diameter cherries in clusters of six to eight fruits. Their tart-fruity flavor makes them very desirable. Indeterminate; 75 days.

Pantano Romanesco: Italian real-red tomatoes with scalloped shape and a meaty interior with deep tomato flavor. Expect great production from these vigorous plants, with 8- to 12-ounce fruits that are good for slicing. Indeterminate; 80 days.

Persimmon: A mid-nineteenth-century tomato with a deep orange color. This indeterminate produces well in short-season gardens, and unlike some of the yellow types, the 1- to 2-pound beefsteak fruits are spicy, with an excellent blend of sugars and acids. Indeterminate; 80 days.

Pineapple: Look for a mélange of sherbet colors, with orange, green, and pinks running through the flesh. This big, meaty tomato with rippled shoulders has hints of pineapple when perfectly ripe. Excellent paired with cheeses. The vines bear lots of 1-pound-plus beauties. Indeterminate; 90 days.

Sainte Lucie: A huge French market beefsteak tomato with fabulous flavor and a meaty, solid flesh. Each vine produces copious quantities of fruits over 1 pound in size. Excellent production and exquisite flavor mark these heirlooms as a garden plus. Indeterminate; 85 days.

Stupice: A Czechoslovakian potato-leaf tomato, early bearing and cold-tolerant, with an abundance of 2-ounce slightly oval red fruits. Their sweet, rich, distinctive flavor

is unusual for such an early-season fruit. Good sliced and lightly dressed with olive oil, salt, and pepper. Easy to grow, either in the ground or in containers. Indeterminate; 52 days.

Sweetie: A cherry tomato that grows on controllable 2-foot-tall vines. Lots of red 1-inch-diameter fruits cover the vines, perfect for salads or snacks. Indeterminate; 75 days.

PINEAPPLE

PANTANO ROMANESCO

EMERALD EVERGREEN

BLACK FROM TULA

PERSIMMON

CHEROKEE PURPLE

GREEN ZEBRA

BLONDKOPFCHEN

STUPICE

MIRABELL

AUNT RUBY'S GERMAN GREEN

BLACK BRANDYWINE

BRANDYWINE OTV

BIG WHITE PINK STRIPE

SAINTE LUCIE

GEORGIA STREAK

FLAMMÉ

SWEETIE

EVA'S PURPLE BALL

GREEN GRAPE

21

TOMATOES + WINE

Pairing food and wine can be fun and delicious, and just a few pointers from the Kendall-Jackson Wine Center will help even the newest oenophile imbibe with enjoyment. Americans are beginning to realize, as have their European counterparts, how misplaced are the mystery and awe surrounding the drinking of wine. Eschew agonizing over the choice of just the right bottle. Disregard what can be the awkward ritual of sniffing the cork. Just relax and savor the first sip of the opened wine. Remember, good dining is as much about the fellowship of sharing the experience with others as it is about the quality of the food and wine.

At the Kendall-Jackson Wine Center, the wine and culinary staff has experimented with pairing many varieties of heirloom tomato with their wines. During the Heirloom Tomato Festival, seminars walk participants through the basic steps of wine tasting and pairing. Participants are first invited to swirl, smell, sip, and taste the wines, with a guided commentary by the Kendall-Jackson staff. Then, the festivalgoers stroll out to Bruschetta Boulevard, where Kendall-Jackson wines are carefully paired with tomato dishes to illustrate how wines contribute to the pleasure of the heirloom tomato table.

Here are the Wine Center staff's suggestions: When sampling a wine new to you, first gently swirl the wine around in the wineglass. Inhale the smell of the perfume that arises from the wine and note its intensity. Observe the color and texture of the wine as it swirls. Light-colored and lightly perfumed white and red wines will likely have an easy, undemanding flavor. Darker, golden-tinted whites or deep red tones indicate richer, probably older wines that may have been aged in oak barrels to introduce stronger flavors of oak and tannin.

After you examine the look and the smell of the wine, take a small sip. Professional wine tasters use the technique of sipping with an intake of breath, to let the wine wash over the entire tongue. Different parts of the tongue register different tastes: The tip of the tongue reacts to sweetness, the sides to sourness, and the center to the taste of salt. The back of the tongue reacts to bitter tastes, such as tannin or flavors from aging wine in oak barrels.

Now, you are ready to taste the wine with a tomato. Executive chef Justin Wangler and the Kendall-Jackson culinary staff have developed a maxim to make pairing a bit easier: Simply match the color of the wines to the color of the tomatoes. To quote the Kendall-Jackson guidelines, "Nature has color-coded fruit and vegetables with the wine best suited to their flavors." So, match up your wines with the colors of tomatoes: Sauvignon Blanc, Chardonnays, and Rieslings do well with white, green, yellow, and orange tomatoes; Pinot Noirs, Merlots, Cabernet Sauvignons, and Zinfandels pair with pinks, reds, and blacks.

These general guidelines work because white, yellow, and orange tomatoes have less acid and more sugar than red-, pink-, and black-fruiting varieties. White wines match the flavors of light-colored tomatoes, with their lower acid balance, while red, pink, and black tomatoes have deeper flavors with more acid to balance their sugars, resulting in richer, bolder tastes.

Chardonnay: A medium-bodied wine with peach, pineapple, vanilla, and red-apple flavors that pair with white, yellow, and green tomatoes. The richer flavor of this wine sings when coupled with Persimmon or Pineapple heirlooms, yellow-orange tomatoes with deep fruity overtones. Chardonnay also works with recipes that combine tomatoes with the smoky flavor of bacon, a match for its own barrel-aged oak hints.

Riesling: This wine goes well with spicy tomato dishes as well as grilled meats and vegetables. Don't discount Rieslings due to their reputation as overly sweet wines, because many have a dry finish. Because of the fact that some of the sugar in the wine has not been converted to alcohol, even the driest are lower in alcohol and excellent for lunch or with hors d'oeuvres. In general, Rieslings are light- to medium-bodied wines with apricot, honeysuckle, and pear flavors that stand up to highly seasoned dishes. One of the best of Bruschetta Boulevard's recipes pairs Riesling with orange tomatoes with chilies, coconut, Indian spices, and cilantro. Spicy salsas made with a mixture of Flammé, Georgia Streak, and chilies would go well with a chilled dry Riesling.

Sauvignon Blanc: This white wine is refreshing and light-bodied, with tropical fruit flavors and notes of fig and grass. Consequently, Sauvignon Blanc pairs with tomato varieties such as Green Grape, Blondkopfchen, or any of the yellow tomatoes that have citrusy flavors with lots of sugar and not much acid. Sauvignon Blanc matches well with the flavor of basil, so light-colored tomatoes with a basil dressing are an appealing combination to serve with this wine.

Cabernet Sauvignon: One of the Kendall-Jackson culinary team's special recipes for Bruschetta Boulevard features Cabernet Sauvignon teamed with Black Brandywine Tomato Jam Bruschetta. The tomatoes are slow cooked with sugar, an ounce of bitter chocolate, and hints of cinnamon until they reach a jam consistency. The sweet mixture tops walnut bread frosted with blue cheese. The Cabernet must stand up to all the rich flavors of the bruschetta, and thanks to the complexity of its makeup, it does. The underriding black cherry, blackberry, and oak flavors of the Cabernet match the stewed tomatoes and underscore the blue cheese and walnut bread. The hearty flavors of Cabernet Sauvignon cry out for pairing with grilled meats, game, or roasts.

Merlot: A Merlot is the perfect accompaniment to an easy Friday-night supper of grilled steak with a salad of Black Brandywine tomatoes. Merlot, a medium- to heavy-bodied wine, has the black cherry, plum, and raspberry undertones that will complement the deep-seated gusto of rich-red and dark-skinned tomatoes. Because of the hint of bell peppers in this wine's flavor profile, a glass of Merlot harmonizes well with a tomato and red or green pepper salad.

Pinot Noir: Pink, red, and black tomatoes call for heavier-bodied, richer wines to stand up to their complex harmony of sugar and acid. Pinot, like Syrah, has less tannin and may be more enjoyable for red-wine drinkers on warm summer days or nights than a heavier-bodied Cabernet Sauvignon. A Pinot Noir, with its flavors of red cherry, strawberry, and hearth smoke, matches well with pink and red tomatoes, as well as deeper-colored types like Eva's Purple Ball or Brandywine OTV. The fruity tones of Pinot Noir suggest unusual pairings such as Pinot with a tomato, watermelon, and basil bruschetta.

Syrah: This heavy-bodied wine with its black cherry, currant, jam, spice, and tobacco tones has the punch to stand up to complex recipes with strong flavors. You might set out a platter of blue cheese with sliced full-bodied, dark-skinned Black From Tula tomatoes. Open a Syrah to drink with tomatoes cooked into a silky red barbecue sauce, or try the Cherokee Purple BLT that is so popular during the Kendall-Jackson festival.

Zinfandel: Zinfandel wines also stand up to hearty, full-flavored dishes. A dish of stewed tomatoes or a rich pasta sauce made with Pantano Romanesco meaty tomatoes would be terrific companioned with a Zinfandel. Just as good would be a glass of Zinfandel to sip alongside grilled meats accompanied with grilled Black Brandywine tomatoes topped with rosemary butter.

COOKING WITH HEIRLOOM TOMATOES

Bert Greene, a cooking school teacher, cookbook author, and syndicated food columnist during the 1980s, used to say that the color of a ripe tomato should be somewhere between "a fire engine and a field of poppies." With the surge in varieties of heirloom tomatoes decked out in rainbow shades of green, yellow, orange, purple, pink, and cream, that statement has become outdated. Today, you need new guidelines to choose the tastiest ripe green, bicolor, white, yellow, orange, or black tomatoes.

● ● ● Choosing and Storing Tomatoes

Trust your senses: a ripe tomato will have the classic winelike tomato perfume, and it will feel heavy, with a slight give when gently squeezed. The tomato should be unblemished, although lighter shoulders and cracks around the stem won't affect the taste. The color should be rich and intense, as tomatoes ripen from the inside out. Any hue of the green of an unripe tomato indicates it has not yet developed its best flavor. Truly ripe green tomatoes will have a yellowish hue.

If you are uncertain, ask your vendor at the farmers' market or the produce manager at your store for assistance. Many vendors will slice a tomato to give you a sample taste. Educate yourself at home, smelling, feeling, and sampling—a pleasant experience, not a bit like work. Try dipping your test tomatoes into a saucer of fruity olive oil and sprinkling a pinch of salt and a grind of pepper over them to see how the flavors expand. In your own garden, pick tomatoes as they ripen for the deepest flavor and taste. The depth of their color and a soft give when squeezed gently indicate their ripeness. Of course, one of the most delicious ways to eat a tomato is to pluck it off the vine, warm from the sun, and pop it into your mouth.

For storage, conquer the impulse to refrigerate tomatoes. The tomato taste depends on a flavor compound, (Z)-3-dexemal, that disappears when the fruit is stored in an environment colder than 50°F. To preserve their true flavor, arrange your tomatoes in colorful bowls on your counters and eat them within two or three days. Slightly unripe tomatoes usually ripen within four to five days on a countertop out of direct sunlight. The joy of tomatoes is eating them within the week of their being picked.

Tools of the Trade

There are a few tools that make the preparation of tomatoes a bit easier and quicker. One of the best is a good serrated knife. The rippling blade of this kind of knife bites into the smooth skin of a tomato and makes excellent slices, thick or thin. For plum or cherry tomatoes, a smaller knife is called for, either a paring knife or a small serrated knife. Another handy tool for tomatoes is a stainless-steel sieve, a food mill, or a tomato/food strainer. Any of these will allow you to create a smooth purée from just-cooked tomatoes by straining out the skins and seeds. Once you have made the purée, you can cook it over low heat to thicken it into tomato paste, or season it and use it as a sauce for pasta or vegetables.

Basic Techniques

Stemming and coring: Large tomatoes have a tough stem and a dense core, designed by nature to keep the fruit hanging on the vine and to deliver nourishment for its growth. Smaller tomatoes, such as plums and cherries, have a softer, edible core and need no extra preparation. For larger tomatoes, use a sharp paring knife or an apple corer to cut out the stem and core. Insert the knife or corer into the center of the fruit and turn the tomato in your hand around the cutting tool. You may need to cut off the woody cracked or hard green shoulders of some tomatoes. For small fruits, simple tug out the stem.

Peeling: When serving sliced tomatoes with tender peels, many cooks prefer to leave the peel on. However, some cooks consider the curls of peels in cooked tomato dishes unattractive. To remove the peel, first bring a large pot of water to a boil. Have handy a large pot of ice water. Stem the tomato and make a shallow X on the bottom of the fruit. Blanch the tomato in the boiling water for 15 to 30 seconds. Using a slotted spoon or wire skimmer, transfer the tomato to the ice water. With the tip of a paring knife or your fingers, slide off the tomato peel. If the peel doesn't come off easily, blanch the tomato again.

Slicing: A very sharp knife or a knife with a serrated blade is the easiest tool for slicing tomatoes. Sometimes you may need to insert the point of the blade to get started through the skin.

Seeding: Tomato seeds become bitter when cooked, and some cooks think they spoil the appearance of a sauce. To remove them, slice the tomato in half crosswise. Turn the tomato half upside down over the sink and shake it to remove the seeds. Or, you can scoop out the seeds with a spoon, or, as Italian cooks do, with your forefinger.

● ● ● Basic Tomato Recipes

The following simple recipes form the basis of any cook's tomato repertoire.

Tomato Concassé

This tomato preparation is the basis for many cooked and raw sauces. Peel and seed tomatoes (see facing page). Using a sharp knife, slice and then chop the tomatoes into a fine dice.

Tomato Coulis

This lightly cooked tomato sauce is excellent as topping for pasta, pizza, fish, or grilled vegetables.

> 3 tablespoons extra-virgin olive oil
> 2 garlic cloves, minced
> 1 pound ripe tomatoes, peeled and seeded
>   (see facing page)
> 2 basil sprigs
> Pinch of salt
> Pinch of sugar (optional)

In a heavy, medium saucepan, heat the olive oil over low heat and sauté the garlic until fragrant, about 1 minute. Add the tomatoes, basil, salt, and sugar and increase the heat to high. Cook, stirring frequently, until the tomatoes begin to soften, about 2 minutes. Remove from the heat and discard the basil. Press the tomatoes through a sieve into a bowl using the back of a large spoon. Let cool. Use now, or cover and refrigerate for up to 4 days. *Makes about 2 cups*

Tomato Water

This pure, clear tomato juice is the distillation of the tomato taste. Use it to intensify the tomato flavor in any recipe.

> 1 pound ripe tomatoes, chopped

Place the tomatoes in a sieve set over a bowl and let drain for about 2 hours, or until the tomatoes stop dripping. To further clarify the tomato water, strain it through cheesecloth or a coffee filter. Use the drained tomatoes in another recipe; a sauce made with them will be less watery than if made with undrained tomatoes. *Makes about ½ cup*

Roasted Tomato Purée

Using a tomato/food strainer, strain chopped tomatoes to remove the peels and seeds. Or, prepare tomato concassé. Lightly coat a rimmed baking sheet or roasting pan with olive oil. Layer with the puréed or diced tomatoes. Cook in a preheated 350°F oven about 2 hours, or until it has thickened to a purée consistency, about 2 hours. Let cool. Use now, or cover and refrigerate for up to 5 days. Or, pour into resealable plastic freezer bags and freeze for up to 6 months.

Oven-Dried Tomatoes

Use your very ripest tomatoes to oven-dry them at home. When dried, their taste intensifies all the best flavors of fully ripened tomatoes, and they are much more flavorful than store-bought varieties.

2 to 3 pounds of cherry or plum tomatoes or

5 pounds full-size tomatoes

(enough to fill 2 baking sheets)

Salt

Olive or canola oil

Cut the cherry or plum tomatoes in half. Salt them lightly on the cut side. Arrange them cut-side down on oiled baking sheets, making sure they do not touch. If using full-size tomatoes, cut them crosswise into thin slices, and salt them lightly. Arrange the slices on oiled baking sheets, making sure they do not touch. You will have two or three baking sheets, depending upon the size of the tomatoes.

Preheat the oven to the lowest setting or 150°F. Cook the tomatoes in the oven until their color darkens and they feel dry to the touch and still supple, about 6 to 8 hours. Any damp spots will mold, so continue to cook the tomatoes until they are fully dried. Store the dry tomatoes in a cool, dark place in sealed plastic bags or glass jars.

To use, drop the dried tomatoes into stews or sauces. To soften the slices, drop them into boiling water for 30 seconds to 1 minute. Repeat until the desired softness is reached and drain. If you wish, cover the softened tomatoes with olive oil and store in a tightly sealed container in the refrigerator for 2 to 3 months. *Makes about 1 quart*

● ● ● Freezing the Harvest for Quick Storage

Gardeners overwhelmed with the bounty of a late-summer harvest can freeze their excess tomatoes. In January, when winter winds, ice, and snow make September's warmth a tenuous memory, those tomatoes can rekindle summer's delight in a fragrant dish, and their taste will be far superior to that of commercial canned products.

If you are faced with buckets of perfectly ripe tomatoes and not a lot of time, the simplest preservation technique is to slip them, whole, into resealable plastic freezer bags and freeze them for later use. When you are ready to use the tomatoes, dunk them, still frozen, into boiling hot water, and their skins will slip off instantly.

You can also freeze leftover tomato sauce in ice cube trays. Extract the cubes and store them in plastic freezer bags. Pop a cube into a pot of cooking food for a tomato hit.

SALSAS + BRUSCHETTAS

HEIRLOOM TOMATO BLOODY MARY SHRIMP SALSA

● ● ●

Zesty homemade roasted-tomato Bloody Mary mix is added to a fresh tomato salsa with shrimp
to create a dish reminiscent of the Mexican shrimp cocktails served in tall glasses. Regardless of its provenance,
it will have your guests hovering around it. —Chef Michael Dunn, Yankee Pier restaurant

2 large heirloom tomatoes, finely diced

12 ounces bay (cocktail) shrimp

1 small red onion, finely diced

1 pasilla chili, seeded and finely diced

¼ cup chopped fresh cilantro

2 tablespoons sliced green onion

½ cup Roasted Tomato Bloody Mary Mix (page 47)

1 tablespoon fresh lemon juice

1½ teaspoons fresh lime juice

Salt and freshly ground pepper to taste

Fresh tortilla chips for serving

Wine Pairing: Sauvignon Blanc

In a medium bowl, combine the tomatoes, shrimp, onion, chili, cilantro, green onion, Bloody Mary mix, and lemon and lime juices; toss well with a spoon. Season with salt and pepper. Serve with tortilla chips. *Serves 4 to 6*

Black Brandywine Tomato Jam and Blue Cheese Bruschetta

● ● ⬤

Rich, dark, and full-bodied Black Brandywine tomatoes, simmered slowly for hours with saba vinegar (a sweet syrup made from the must of Trebbiano grapes), cinnamon, and a touch of bittersweet chocolate, are paired with blue cheese and walnut bread. This astonishing array of ingredients blends together with amazing results. —Kendall-Jackson Culinary Team

5 pounds Black Brandywine tomatoes, halved

2 tablespoons light olive oil, such as Carapelli brand

1/2 cup Kendall-Jackson Vintner's Reserve Cabernet wine or other dry red wine

3 tablespoons packed brown sugar

2 tablespoons saba vinegar or aged balsamic vinegar

1/2 stick cinnamon

1 ounce bittersweet chocolate

Pinch of sea salt

6 to 8 slices walnut bread, toasted

1 pound blue cheese, such as Rogue River Oregon Blue

Wine Pairing: Cabernet Sauvignon

Preheat the oven to 400°F. Brush the cut sides of the tomatoes with the olive oil. Place, cut side down, on a baking sheet and roast until charred and soft, 45 minutes to 1 hour. In a food mill, blender, or food processor, purée the tomatoes and any juice they have exuded.

In a large, heavy nonreactive saucepan, combine the tomato purée, wine, brown sugar, saba vinegar, and cinnamon stick. Bring to a boil, reduce the heat to a low simmer, and stir constantly until the tomatoes have reached a jamlike consistency, about 1 1/2 hours. Remove and discard the cinnamon stick. Add the chocolate and salt and stir until the chocolate melts. Remove from the heat and let cool.

To serve, spread the jam on the toasted walnut bread and top with a slice of blue cheese. *Serves 6 to 8*

AUNT RUBY'S GREEN GERMAN TOMATO RELISH AND GOAT CHEESE BRUSCHETTA

● ● ●

Sweet, ripe green heirloom tomatoes combined with tomatillos, mild vinegar, and olive oil serve to balance the buttery flavor of goat cheese. The vibrant green relish is a colorful addition to other summer antipasti, or it can be used alone to accompany a seafood entrée. —Kendall-Jackson Culinary Team

1 pound tomatillos, husked and blanched for 2 to 3 minutes

3 tablespoons light olive oil

2 pounds Aunt Ruby's Green German heirloom tomatoes, peeled, seeded (see page 28), and cut into ½-inch dice

2 tablespoons Champagne vinegar

¼ cup torn or julienned fresh basil leaves

Sea salt and freshly ground pepper to taste

6 to 8 thin diagonal baguette slices, toasted

4 ounces fresh goat cheese, such as Redwood Hill Farm

Wine Pairing: Sauvignon Blanc

In a blender or food processor, process the tomatillos to a smooth purée. In a large nonreactive sauté pan, heat 2 tablespoons of the olive oil over high heat, add the tomatoes, and sauté for 1 minute, then add the vinegar and tomatillo purée. Strain the mixture through a fine-mesh sieve set over a bowl. Reserve the tomatoes in another bowl and return the juice to the sauté pan. Cook the juice over high heat to reduce to a syrup, about 5 minutes. Remove from the heat and let cool slightly. Stir the reduced juice, basil, and remaining 1 tablespoon olive oil into the tomatoes and season with salt and pepper.

To serve, spoon the relish onto the toasted baguette slices and garnish with slices of goat cheese. *Serves 6 to 8*

EVA'S PURPLE BALL TOMATO AND WATERMELON BRUSCHETTA

• • •

These flavorful pink heirloom tomatoes combine well with rich, almost chocolaty opal basil and sweet seedless watermelon. The tangy-sweet bruschetta topping can also be served as an accompaniment to grilled fish or chicken. —Kendall-Jackson Culinary Team

2 pounds Eva's Purple Ball heirloom tomatoes, seeded (see page 28) and cut into $\frac{1}{2}$-inch dice

$1\frac{1}{2}$ pounds seedless red watermelon, peeled and cut into $\frac{1}{2}$-inch dice (about 3 cups)

3 tablespoons torn or thinly sliced fresh opal basil

$1\frac{1}{2}$ tablespoons vincotto (Italian sweet vinegar)

1 tablespoon light olive oil

Sea salt to taste

6 to 8 slices sourdough bread, toasted

Wine Pairing: Pinot Noir

In a bowl, toss the tomatoes, watermelon, basil, vincotto, and olive oil together. Season with salt. To serve, spoon onto the toasted sourdough bread slices. *Serves 6 to 8*

HAWAIIAN PINEAPPLE TOMATO BRUSCHETTA

• • •

The gentle acidity of the Hawaiian Pineapple tomato is perfectly balanced with sweet corn and fresh tarragon. You can substitute any of the sweet yellow or orange heirloom tomatoes, such as Persimmon or Yellow Brandywine, in this dish. —Kendall-Jackson Culinary Team

3 pounds Hawaiian Pineapple tomatoes, cut into $\frac{3}{8}$-inch dice

1 tablespoon Chardonnay vinegar

$\frac{1}{4}$ cup extra-virgin olive oil

$1\frac{1}{2}$ cups corn kernels (about 3 ears)

$1\frac{1}{2}$ tablespoons minced fresh tarragon

Salt and freshly ground pepper to taste

6 to 8 thin slices French bread, toasted

Wine Pairing: Chardonnay

Drain the diced tomatoes in a sieve or colander set over a bowl for a few minutes to catch the juice. In a large bowl, whisk the reserved tomato juice, vinegar, and olive oil together. Add the tomatoes, corn, and tarragon; toss gently and season with salt and pepper. Serve on the toasted French bread. *Serves 6 to 8*

Right: Eva's Purple Ball Tomato and Watermelon Bruschetta

Indian-Spiced Orange Tomato, Chili, and Coconut Bruschetta

• • •

Spicy foods are prescribed in hot weather to cool down the body. Here, heirloom orange tomatoes present a perfect blend of acid, sugar, and richness when paired with an East Indian blend of chilies and coconut. —Kendall-Jackson Culinary Team

2 tablespoons extra-virgin olive oil

4 green onions, including light green parts, thinly sliced

4 garlic cloves, minced

1 jalapeño chili, seeded and minced

2 teaspoons mustard seeds

1 teaspoon ground turmeric

5 pounds orange heirloom tomatoes, seeded
(see page 28) and cut into 1/2-inch dice

1 teaspoon sugar

Salt and freshly ground pepper to taste

6 to 8 thin slices French bread, toasted

1/2 cup sweetened coconut flakes, toasted (see note)

1/4 cup chopped fresh cilantro

Wine Pairing: Riesling

In a large nonreactive sauté pan, heat the olive oil over medium heat. Add the green onions, garlic, chili, mustard seeds, and turmeric and sauté until fragrant, about 1 minute. Add the tomatoes and cook just until they begin to release their juices, about 1 minute. Remove the pan from the heat. Stir in the sugar, season with salt and pepper, and let cool.

To serve, drain off the excess liquid and spoon the tomatoes onto the toasted French bread. Garnish with the toasted coconut and cilantro. *Serves 6 to 8*

Note: To toast coconut, spread the coconut in an even layer on a baking sheet. Toast in a preheated 325°F oven, stirring occasionally, until golden, about 10 minutes.

Left to right: Hawaiian Pineapple Tomato Bruschetta (page 38); Indian-Spiced Orange Tomato, Chili, and Coconut Bruschetta (this page); and Aunt Ruby's Green German Tomato Relish and Goat Cheese Bruschetta (page 37)

ROASTED PEPPER, MUSHROOM, AND SUN-DRIED TOMATO COMPOTE

● ● ●

A plain roast chicken paired with this compote becomes a lively rumba of flavors.
Also try this as a topping for bruschetta—perfect as a snack or for hors d'oeuvres. —Chef Jeffrey Madura, John Ash & Co.

½ cup oven-dried yellow tomatoes (page 30) or
    dry-packed sun-dried tomatoes

6 ounces shiitake mushrooms, stemmed, or
    a mixture of mushrooms

4 tablespoons olive oil

3 tablespoons balsamic vinegar

3 rosemary sprigs

3 thyme sprigs

3 red and 3 yellow bell peppers, roasted, seeded, and
    julienned (see note)

8 cloves garlic, thinly sliced

¼ cup chopped fresh basil

½ teaspoon kosher salt

Freshly ground pepper to taste

Wine Pairing: Syrah

In a nonreactive pot of boiling water, blanch the tomatoes until pliable but not mushy, about 2 minutes. Drain and set aside.

Cut the mushrooms into quarters. In a medium bowl, toss the mushrooms with 3 tablespoons of the olive oil and the balsamic vinegar.

In a large nonreactive sauté pan, heat the remaining 1 tablespoon olive oil until almost smoking. Add the mushrooms, rosemary, and thyme and sauté until the mushrooms are tender but not limp, 3 to 5 minutes. Add the tomatoes, bell peppers, garlic, basil, salt, and pepper and cook, stirring occasionally, for 5 minutes. Remove from the heat and let stand, covered, for 1 hour. Remove the herb sprigs before serving. *Serves 4*

Note: To roast and seed bell peppers, place the peppers directly on the open flame of a stove-top burner or place them on a tray under a pre-heated broiler about 2 inches from the heat source. Turn the peppers occasionally with a pair of tongs until the skin is evenly blistered and blackened. Place the peppers in a paper bag or a bowl with a lid and let cool for about 10 minutes. Rub off the skins with your fingers. Pull off and discard the stems and seeds.

FIVE-MINUTE BRANDYWINE TOMATO SAUCE

• • •

This quick, delicious sauce is wonderful to have on hand for instant menu fixes and unexpected dinner guests all year long. The Brandywine's sweet, deep flavors make this fresh tomato sauce work. You could substitute any beefsteak heirloom with equally rich flavors, such as Mortgage Lifter or Georgia Streak. Whip out the sauce for fresh pasta or grilled fish, meats, or vegetables, and freeze some extra for a burst of summer flavor when fresh tomatoes are out of season. —Chef John Besh, Restaurant August

¼ cup extra-virgin olive oil

2½ pounds very ripe Brandywine tomatoes, quartered

3 cloves garlic, thinly sliced

2 teaspoons red pepper flakes

1 teaspoon sugar

Pinch of sea salt

1 tablespoon chopped fresh basil

Salt and freshly ground pepper to taste

Wine Pairing: Zinfandel

In a large nonreactive pot, heat the olive oil over high heat. Add the tomatoes and stir until heated through and well coated with oil, 3 to 4 minutes. Add the garlic, red pepper flakes, sugar, and sea salt. Bring to a boil, then reduce the heat to medium and cook for 5 minutes, stirring occasionally. Stir in the basil and remove from the heat. Let cool slightly. In a food mill, blender, or food processor, purée the tomato mixture. Season with salt and pepper. Store in the refrigerator in a sealed plastic container for up to 1 week or freeze in a sealed plastic bag or plastic container for up to 2 months. *Makes 4 cups*

SOUPS + BEVERAGES

HOOSIER TOMATO JUICE

● ● ●

A wonder like this could only come about in a world with an abundance of tomatoes. Our family in Indiana always canned their own juice at the end of August, the height of the tomato season there. The juice was served in small glasses as an appetizer, with just a little salt, pepper, and lemon juice added. All-red juice is classic, but in California we tend to make ours with perfectly delicious, but less-than-perfect-looking heirloom tomatoes (saving the perfect ones for slicing). It's an Indiana truism: Any tomato that tastes good will make good juice.

Drink the chilled juice straight up, or over ice. Spice it to taste with lime or lemon, pepper, and/or hot pepper sauce, and definitely consider using it in Bloody Marys. Leftover juice freezes well and makes a nice base for a light vegetable soup. —Chef Carrie Brown, Jimtown Store

5 pounds perfectly ripe, utterly flavorful tomatoes
(size, shape, and color are not as important as taste)
¼ teaspoon salt

One at a time, holding them over a bowl to catch all their juices, core the tomatoes, discard the cores, and chop the flesh into ½-inch pieces. In a large nonreactive pot, combine the tomatoes and juices and bring to a simmer. Cook, stirring once or twice, until the tomatoes have released all their juices, about 3 minutes.

Set a sieve over a bowl. Working in batches, press on the tomatoes with the back of a large spoon to force the juice through into the bowl. Discard the seeds and peels. Wipe the pan clean and return the juice to it. Bring to a boil over medium heat, then reduce the heat slightly and simmer briskly, uncovered, to reduce to 4 cups, 8 to 10 minutes. Stir in the salt, remove from the heat, and let cool to room temperature. Cover and refrigerate until cold, at least 2 hours. Serve now, or cover and refrigerate for up to 2 days, or freeze for up to 1 month. *Makes 4 cups*

Note: The step of simmering the juice to reduce it can be omitted if the juice is intensely flavorful as is, or you don't particularly desire thick juice.

ROASTED HEIRLOOM TOMATO BLOODY MARY

• • •

Making your own roasted-tomato Bloody Mary mix is easy, and the flavor is beyond comparison with store-bought mixes.
—Chef Michael Dunn, Yankee Pier restaurant

Cocktail ice cubes for shaking

1 1/2 ounces vodka

3 ounces Roasted Tomato Bloody Mary Mix
    (recipe follows)

Squeeze of fresh lemon juice

1/2 teaspoon Worcestershire sauce

2 drops of Tabasco sauce

Ice cubes for serving

Celery salt to taste

1 lime wedge for garnish

In a cocktail shaker filled with cocktail ice cubes, combine the vodka, Bloody Mary mix, lemon juice, Worcestershire sauce, and Tabasco sauce. Shake well and strain into an old-fashioned glass over ice cubes. Add celery salt and garnish with the lime wedge. *Serves 1*

ROASTED TOMATO BLOODY MARY MIX

2 red heirloom tomatoes, quartered

1/2 onion, cut into large dice

1 jalapeño chili, stemmed

1/4 cup vodka

1/4 cup tomato water (page 29)

2 tablespoons chopped fresh cilantro

Salt and freshly ground pepper to taste

Fresh lemon juice to taste

Preheat the oven to 350°F. Spread the tomatoes, onion, and chili in a non-reactive roasting pan in one layer and roast for about 25 minutes, or until lightly browned. Add the vodka and tomato water to the pan and roast for another 15 minutes. Transfer the roasted vegetables to a blender, add the cilantro, and purée until smooth. Season with salt, pepper, and lemon juice. Refrigerate until cold, at least 2 hours, or up to 2 days. *Makes 2 cups*

TOMATO-WATERMELON AGUA FRESCA

● ● ●

We developed this beautiful reddish pink drink to serve at Kendall-Jackson's annual tomato festival and were rewarded with rave reviews. It's sheer refreshment, a startling combination that usually elicits a wondrous "Ahhh" and questions of "How did you ever think of that?" And yet, why not? Two red fruits at their mutual height-of-summer peaks of perfection really ought to taste great together. —Chef Carrie Brown, Jimtown Store

Mint Syrup

½ cup packed fresh mint leaves

¾ cup sugar

¾ cup water

6 pounds seedless watermelon, peeled and cut into chunks

4 cups Hoosier Tomato Juice (page 46) or commercial bottled tomato juice

⅓ cup fresh lime juice

½ teaspoon kosher salt

Ice cubes for serving

Mint sprigs for garnish (optional)

Thin watermelon wedges, cherry tomatoes, and lime wedges for garnish (optional)

Sea salt for serving (optional)

To make the mint syrup: Put the mint leaves in a medium bowl. In a small saucepan, combine the sugar and water. Bring to a boil over medium heat. Reduce the heat to low and simmer until the sugar dissolves. Pour the syrup over the mint leaves. Set aside and let cool to room temperature. Strain through a fine-mesh sieve, pushing on the leaves with the back of a large spoon. Use now, or cover and refrigerate for up to 3 weeks.

In a blender, working in batches, purée the watermelon until fairly smooth. Strain out any large chunks and measure out 5 cups juice. In a nonreactive container, combine the watermelon juice, tomato juice, mint syrup, lime juice, and salt. Stir to blend. Cover and refrigerate until very cold, at least 2 hours.

To serve, pour the agua fresca over ice in tall glasses. Garnish each with a mint sprig, if desired.

To add a festive garnish, if desired, slide a small wedge of melon, a cherry tomato, and a wedge of lime onto skewers and insert one into each glass. You might also want to set a small dish of sea salt on the drinks tray and let guests add a pinch, to taste, to their drinks. *Makes 9 cups; serves 6*

COLD GOLDEN TOMATO SOUP
WITH SHARLYN MELON AND BASIL ESSENCE

● ● ●

The affinity between ripe melons and yellow heirloom tomatoes makes sense when you consider that they both have a fruity, sweetly perfumed depth of flavor. Try this soup as a first course for a summer Sunday brunch. —Chef Vincent Herrera, Lark Creek Inn at Walnut Creek

¼ cup sugar

¼ cup water

1-inch piece fresh ginger, peeled and grated or minced

2 pounds Persimmon or Golden Peach tomatoes, chopped

½ cup fresh basil leaves, plus 6 leaves for frying

¼ cup snipped fresh chives

1 tablespoon fresh lemon juice

¼ cup olive oil, plus olive oil for frying

1 Sharlyn melon or other orange-fleshed melon such as cantaloupe or Galia

Salt and freshly ground pepper to taste

Wine Pairing: Chardonnay

In a small saucepan, combine the sugar, water, and ginger and bring to a boil over medium heat. Reduce the heat to low and simmer until the sugar dissolves. Remove from the heat and let cool completely. Strain through a fine-mesh sieve into a bowl and set aside.

In a food mill, blender, or food processor, purée the tomatoes. Strain through a fine-mesh sieve into a large bowl. Add the ginger syrup and refrigerate for at least 30 minutes.

In a blender, purée the ½ cup basil, the chives, and the lemon juice with the ¼ cup olive oil. Strain through a fine-mesh sieve and set aside.

Use a melon baller to scoop twenty 1-inch-diameter balls from the melon, working over a bowl to catch the melon juice. Add the juice to the tomato soup and season the soup with salt and pepper.

In a small sauté pan, heat about ½ inch olive oil over medium heat until a basil leaf sizzles when you dip the tip in the oil. Fry the basil leaves until they stop sizzling, about 30 seconds. Using a slotted spoon, transfer to paper towels to drain. The leaves will crisp as they cool.

To serve, pile 5 melon balls in the center of each bowl and slowly ladle tomato soup around them. Drizzle basil oil around the melon balls and garnish each bowl with a fried basil leaf. *Serves 4*

CHILLED CREOLE TOMATO SOUP WITH TAPENADE

● ● ●

This is one of my favorite ways to begin a dinner on a hot summer night. Many also enjoy this as a starter to a summer brunch.
—Chef John Besh, Restaurant August

1 small ancho chili
¼ cup extra-virgin olive oil
3 garlic cloves, crushed
3 pounds ripe heirloom tomatoes, coarsely chopped
2 red bell peppers, seeded and chopped
2 tablespoons sherry vinegar
½ cup fresh basil leaves, torn
1 teaspoon fresh thyme leaves
Salt and freshly ground pepper to taste
Sugar to taste (optional)

Tapenade
¼ cup pitted black olives
2 garlic cloves
2 oil-packed anchovy fillets (optional)
Juice of ½ lemon
½ cup extra-virgin olive oil

Wine Pairing: Syrah

Soak the ancho chili in very hot water until soft, about 5 minutes. Remove the stem and seeds. In a large nonreactive pot, heat the olive oil over medium-high heat and sauté the garlic until it sizzles but does not brown, about 2 minutes. Add the tomatoes and bell peppers, reduce the heat to medium, and simmer, stirring occasionally, until the peppers are soft, about 15 minutes. Add the vinegar, basil, and thyme and stir for 2 to 3 minutes. Using a food mill, blender, or food processor, purée the mixture (in batches, if necessary). Strain through a medium-mesh sieve into a large bowl. Season with salt and pepper. If necessary, a small amount of sugar may be added; however, most ripe heirloom tomatoes have enough natural sugar to balance out the acidity in this dish. Cover and refrigerate for at least 2 hours before serving.

To make the tapenade: In a food processor, purée the olives, garlic, anchovies (if using), and lemon juice. With the machine running, gradually add the olive oil.

To serve, ladle into chilled shallow soup bowls and garnish each serving with a spoonful of tapenade. *Serves 6*

SPICY HEIRLOOM TOMATO SOUP

• • •

We like to serve this spicy soup with grilled cheese sandwiches made with Bellwether Farms Carmody cheese.
—Chefs Duskie Estes and John Stewart, Zazu restaurant

1 carrot, peeled and coarsely chopped

1 onion, coarsely chopped

1 stalk celery, coarsely chopped

¼ cup olive oil

5 garlic cloves

¼ teaspoon red pepper flakes, or to taste

2 pounds heirloom tomatoes, peeled and seeded
   (see page 28)

2 cups water

2 teaspoons kosher salt

Extra-virgin olive oil for drizzling

Wine Pairing: Pinot Noir or Chardonnay if served with grilled cheese sandwiches

In a food processor, combine the carrot, onion, and celery and finely chop. In a large nonreactive saucepan, heat the olive oil over medium-high heat and sauté the garlic until golden and fragrant, about 5 minutes. Add the chopped vegetables and red pepper flakes. Sauté for about 7 minutes, or until fragrant and starting to color. Add the tomatoes, water, and salt. Reduce the heat to medium-low and simmer for about 20 minutes. Purée with an immersion blender, stand blender, or food mill. Taste and adjust the seasoning.

To serve, ladle into warmed shallow soup bowls and garnish each serving with a drizzle of extra-virgin olive oil. *Serves 6*

Tomato Bisque

● ● ●

We are very proud of this recipe, which was the winner of the fourth annual Kendall-Jackson Tomato Festival People's Choice Award for Best Tomato Dish. It is the recipe most often requested by our customers and the most popular soup at our gourmet take-out. —Chef Amber Balshaw, Preferred Sonoma Caterers

8 tablespoons unsalted butter

1/2 cup chopped onion

1 1/2 teaspoons minced fresh dill, plus more for garnish

2 pounds heirloom tomatoes, chopped

4 cups chicken or vegetable broth

2 tablespoons all-purpose flour

1 1/4 cups heavy cream

2/3 cup half-and-half

1/4 cup minced fresh flat-leaf parsley

1/4 cup honey

Salt and freshly ground pepper to taste

Wine Pairing: Sauvignon Blanc

In a large nonreactive pot, melt 6 tablespoons of the butter over medium heat and sauté the onion and the 1 1/2 teaspoons dill until the onion is translucent, about 5 minutes. Add the tomatoes and broth, bring to a simmer, and remove from the heat.

In a small saucepan, melt the remaining 2 tablespoons butter over medium heat and add the flour, stirring constantly with a wooden spoon for 3 minutes without browning. Add the cream and half-and-half and bring to a boil, stirring occasionally. Reduce the heat to medium-low and simmer for 15 minutes. Stir in the parsley and honey. Remove from the heat. Using an immersion blender, stand blender, or food processor, purée the cream mixture with the tomato-broth mixture (in batches, if necessary). Return the blended soup to the same pot, reheat over low heat, and season with salt and pepper.

To serve, ladle into warmed shallow soup bowls and garnish with dill.
Serves 6 to 8

COUNTRY TOMATO SOUP WITH PARMESAN-CAPER CROSTINI

● ● ●

This recipe might be called "double-tomato soup," for the tomato-rich broth adds an immeasurable, sweet richness to the tomato soup itself. Who could argue with the results of soup made with four pounds of summer-ripe heirloom tomatoes? —Chef Phil Conde, Yankee Pier restaurant

Tomato Stock

1 tablespoon extra-virgin olive oil

1 yellow onion, thinly sliced

2 stalks celery, thinly sliced

1 small carrot, peeled and thinly sliced

3 garlic cloves, thinly sliced

1½ pounds ripe heirloom plum tomatoes, halved, seeded (see page 28), and chopped

6 cups water

1 tablespoon extra-virgin olive oil

1 large red onion, thinly sliced

2 garlic cloves, thinly sliced

2½ pounds ripe heirloom plum tomatoes, halved, seeded (see page 28), and chopped

¼ cup chopped fresh basil

1 teaspoon fresh thyme leaves

1 bay leaf

1½ cups crustless bread cubes, cut from day-old baguette

Salt and freshly ground pepper to taste

To make the tomato stock: In a large nonreactive pot, heat the olive oil over medium heat. Add the yellow onion and stir until translucent, about 5 minutes. Add the celery, carrot, and garlic and cook, stirring occasionally, until softened, about 8 minutes. Add the tomatoes and water. Simmer, uncovered, for 45 minutes. Strain through a fine-mesh sieve and set aside.

In a large nonreactive pot, heat the olive oil over medium heat. Add the red onion and garlic. Cook, stirring constantly, until lightly browned, about 10 minutes. Add the tomatoes, basil, thyme, and bay leaf and cook for 10 minutes, stirring occasionally to help the tomatoes break down and release their juices. Add the tomato stock and bread and simmer, uncovered, for 30 minutes. Remove the bay leaf.

Using an immersion blender, stand blender, or food processor, purée the soup (in batches, if necessary) until smooth. Strain the soup through a medium-mesh sieve into a clean nonreactive pot. Heat over low heat, and season with salt and pepper. Remove from the heat and cover to keep warm.

Parmesan-Caper Crostini

1/2 cup (2 ounces) finely shredded Parmesan cheese

2 tablespoons extra-virgin olive oil

1 tablespoon capers, rinsed and chopped

2 garlic cloves, minced

1 teaspoon grated lemon zest

Salt and freshly ground pepper to taste

Twelve 1/4-inch-thick baguette slices, toasted

1 tablespoon minced fresh flat-leaf parsley for garnish

Wine Pairing: Cabernet Sauvignon

To make the crostini: In a small bowl, stir the Parmesan, olive oil, capers, garlic, and lemon zest together. Season with salt and pepper. Spread onto the toasted baguette slices.

To serve, ladle the soup into warmed shallow bowls. Garnish with the crostini and parsley. *Serves 6*

SALADS + SIDE DISHES

HEIRLOOM TOMATO AND MELON SALAD

● ● ●

The use of melon in a savory course is not new, and you needn't sample a plate of prosciutto-wrapped cantaloupe in a Roman trattoria to know this culinary truth. Another layer of kitchen alchemy is at work in this salad, however, with the addition of honey and lime, transforming the perfume of perfectly ripe melons and tangy cherry tomatoes into something mysterious and ambrosial. Make it in August and September, when both fruits are at their peaks. —Chefs Carrie Brown, John Werner, and Michael McLaughlin, Jimtown Store

2 tablespoons fresh lime juice

1 teaspoon light floral honey, such as wildflower or
    star thistle

1/2 green-fleshed melon, seeded, peeled, and cut into
    1/2-inch chunks (about 3 cups)

1/2 orange-fleshed melon, seeded, peeled, and cut into
    1/2-inch chunks (about 3 cups)

2 pints red and heirloom cherry tomatoes, stemmed,
    all but the smallest halved

1/2 teaspoon kosher salt

1/4 teaspoon cayenne pepper or Tierra Farm's
    chipotle powder

Wine Pairing: Riesling

In a large bowl, whisk the lime juice and honey together. Add the melons and tomatoes and toss to coat. Sprinkle with the salt and cayenne pepper or chipotle powder and toss again. Transfer the salad to a deep platter. Serve now, or let stand for 1 hour to allow the flavors to blend. *Serves 6 to 8*

Variation: For a composed salad, layer slices of large heirloom tomatoes with thin wedges of melon on a platter and drizzle the dressing over the fruits. Sprinkle with salt and cayenne or chipotle powder.

FRIED GREEN TOMATO CAPRESE SALAD
WITH MARJORAM VINAIGRETTE

● ● ●

At the end of summer, when you may have some tomatoes that never got ripe, here is a perfect use for them!
—Chefs Duskie Estes and John Stewart, Zazu restaurant

Marjoram Vinaigrette

2 tablespoons red wine vinegar

1 teaspoon minced shallot

1 teaspoon minced fresh marjoram

1/3 cup extra-virgin olive oil

Kosher salt and freshly ground pepper to taste

1 1/2 cups buttermilk

1/2 teaspoon sweet paprika

1/4 teaspoon cayenne pepper

1 cup all-purpose flour

1 cup cornmeal

4 green tomatoes, sliced 1/3 inch thick crosswise

Olive oil for frying

Kosher salt and freshly ground pepper to taste

8 ounces Bellwether Farms Crescenza cheese, or any
favorite soft cheese such as fresh mozzarella or feta

Wine Pairing: Chardonnay

To make the vinaigrette: In a small bowl, combine the vinegar, shallot, and marjoram. Slowly whisk in the extra-virgin olive oil and season with salt and pepper.

In a shallow bowl or pie pan, combine the buttermilk, paprika, and cayenne. In another shallow bowl or pie pan, combine the flour and cornmeal. With one hand, dip the green tomato slices in buttermilk and then drop them into the flour. With the other hand, turn the slices in the flour mixture to coat; transfer to baking sheets until ready to fry.

Heat 1/4 inch olive oil in 2 large nonreactive sauté pans over medium-high heat. Fry as many tomato slices as will fit comfortably in the pans at one time until golden brown on both sides, about 3 minutes total. Using a slotted metal spatula, transfer to paper towels to drain and season with salt and pepper.

To serve, divide the tomatoes among 4 salad plates and garnish with dollops of the cheese. Ladle about 1 1/2 tablespoons of the marjoram vinaigrette over each plate. *Serves 4*

SOUTHWESTERN HEIRLOOM TOMATO SALAD

• • •

This heirloom tomato salad won the People's Choice Award at the 2003 Kendall-Jackson Heirloom Tomato Festival. Serve it warm or chilled, as an accompaniment to grilled chicken, meat, or fish. —Chef Fred Langley, Langley's on the Green

1 teaspoon cumin seeds

2 tablespoons olive oil

1 garlic clove, minced

1 large heirloom tomato, seeded (see page 28) and diced

2½ cups corn kernels (about 4 large ears)

2 cups cooked black beans, or 1 can (15 ounces) black beans, drained

Kosher salt and freshly ground pepper to taste

Wine Pairing: Chardonnay

In a dry, medium nonreactive sauté pan over high heat, toast the cumin seeds, stirring frequently, until fragrant, about 2 minutes. Let cool and grind in a spice grinder or in a mortar.

In the same pan, heat the olive oil over medium heat. Add the garlic and sauté for 1 minute. Add the tomato and corn kernels and sauté for another minute. Add the black beans and ground cumin and season with salt and pepper. Serve warm, or cover and refrigerate for up to 3 days *Serves 4*

BLT Salad

● ● ●

At Zazu and Bovolo restaurants, John cures our own bacon made from Berkshire pigs. Niman Ranch also makes great bacon; look for it in quality grocery stores. Use the extra dressing on other salads, artichokes, and asparagus. —Chefs Duskie Estes and John Stewart, Zazu restaurant

Leaves from 1 head butter lettuce

2 large heirloom tomatoes, sliced

1 avocado, peeled, pitted, and diced

1 cup Buttermilk Dressing (recipe follows)

8 slices bacon, cooked until crisp, then crumbled

Wine Pairing: Syrah or Merlot

Divide the butter lettuce leaves among 4 salad plates. Top with the tomato slices, sprinkle with the avocado, and drizzle each plate with $1/4$ cup buttermilk dressing. Top each plate with the crumbled bacon. *Serves 4*

Buttermilk Dressing

$1/4$ cup red wine vinegar

1 egg yolk

1 small shallot, coarsely chopped

1 cup virgin olive oil

1 cup buttermilk

2 tablespoons minced fresh flat-leaf parsley

1 teaspoon minced fresh thyme

Kosher salt and freshly ground pepper to taste

In a blender or food processor, blend the red wine vinegar, egg yolk, and shallot. With the machine running, gradually add the olive oil to emulsify. Add the buttermilk, parsley, and thyme and pulse to combine. Season with salt and pepper. Cover and refrigerate leftover dressing for up to 3 days. *Makes 2 cups*

Grilled Heirloom Tomato Salad with Roasted Garlic Purée

● ● ●

The smoky touch of the grill intensifies the sweet flavor of heirloom tomatoes, making them the perfect base for any recipe.
Roasting garlic tames its nature, turning the cloves into a gentle garlic-fragrant butter that can be smeared on toasts.
Here, the rich baked garlic sauce dappled over the arugula complements the nutty flavor of its leaves. This salad could be a vegetarian
lunch dish, but it would also be the perfect companion to grilled meats. —Chef Michael Dunn, Yankee Pier restaurant

Roasted Garlic Purée

5 garlic heads

1/2 cup vegetable broth

2 tablespoons balsamic vinegar

2 tablespoons unsalted butter, cut into small pieces

1 1/2 teaspoons olive oil

Kosher salt and freshly ground pepper to taste

4 large heirloom tomatoes, cut into 1/2-inch-thick
    crosswise slices

2/3 cup olive oil

1/3 cup balsamic vinegar

1 red onion, thinly sliced

4 bunches arugula (about 12 cups)

1 cup (5 ounces) crumbled feta cheese

Salt and freshly ground pepper to taste

Wine Pairing: Pinot Noir

To make the garlic purée: Preheat the oven to 300°F. Cut off the top 1/2 inch of each head of garlic to expose the cloves, and peel away any loose skin. Put the garlic in a small ovenproof casserole or an ovenproof saucepan. Add the vegetable broth and balsamic vinegar. Scatter the butter on top of the garlic, drizzle with the olive oil, and sprinkle with salt and pepper. Cover the pan with a lid or aluminum foil and bake until the cloves are soft and starting to come out of the garlic heads, about 1 hour. Squeeze the garlic out of the heads into a food processor, reserving the cooking liquid. Purée the garlic, adding enough of the reserved liquid to make a thick but pourable purée. If necessary, thin with water or vegetable broth. Season with salt and pepper.

Light a charcoal or wood fire in an outdoor grill, or heat a large grill pan over high heat. Coat the grill grids with oil using an oil-soaked paper towel. Cook the tomatoes for about 1 minute on each side, turning with a metal spatula. Transfer the tomatoes to a plate.

In a large bowl, whisk together the olive oil and balsamic vinegar. Add the onion, arugula, and feta cheese and toss well. Season with salt and pepper.

To serve, divide the tomato slices among 6 salad plates. Pile the arugula salad on top of the tomatoes and drizzle each plate with 2 tablespoons of the roasted garlic purée. *Serves 6*

TOMATO-AVOCADO SALAD WITH GARLIC TOASTS AND CHÈVRE CREAM

● ● ◗

Avocados and tomatoes are always a terrific team, but this recipe adds a few surprising flavor notes.
Make sure to serve it at room temperature to allow all its flavors to mellow and deepen. —Chef Craig Ponsford, Artisan Bakers

4 heirloom tomatoes, cut into ½-inch dice

1 ripe avocado, peeled, halved, and pitted

2 tablespoons lemon-flavored olive oil

Juice of 1 lime

2 garlic cloves, thinly sliced

1 tablespoon chopped fresh cilantro

2 teaspoons minced fresh oregano

1 teaspoon freshly ground pepper

½ teaspoon ground cumin

Kosher salt to taste

Chèvre Cream

½ cup cream cheese

¼ cup fresh goat cheese

¼ cup half-and-half

2 teaspoons chopped fresh cilantro

1 teaspoon minced fresh oregano

1 garlic clove, minced

Salt and freshly ground pepper to taste

Garlic Toasts

2 tablespoons virgin olive oil

1 garlic clove, minced

½ baguette, cut into ¼-inch slices

Salt and freshly ground pepper to taste

Wine Pairing: Cabernet Sauvignon

Put the tomatoes in a large bowl. Cut the avocado halves in half cross-wise, then slice each piece lengthwise into ¼-inch-wide strips. Add the avocado, lemon-flavored olive oil, lime juice, garlic, cilantro, oregano, pepper, and cumin to the diced tomatoes and toss gently but thoroughly. Season with salt. Let sit for 5 minutes and toss again. Taste and adjust the seasoning. Set aside at room temperature.

To make the chèvre cream: In a food processor or a bowl, blend the cream cheese, goat cheese, half-and-half, cilantro, oregano, and garlic together until smooth. Season with salt and pepper. Refrigerate until needed.

To make the garlic toasts: Preheat the oven to 325°F. In medium sauté pan, heat the virgin olive oil over medium heat and sauté the garlic until it starts to sizzle. Toss the baguette slices in the oil mixture until thoroughly coated, then transfer to a baking sheet and sprinkle with salt and pepper on both sides. Toast in the oven until crisp and lightly browned, about 10 minutes.

To serve, put the tomato and avocado salad in a large serving bowl or divide among salad plates. Spread the chèvre cream on the garlic toasts and arrange them on top of or around the salad in a decorative fashion. *Serves 4 to 6*

TOMATO SFORMATINO

● ● ●

Sformatino means "little unmolded thing" in Italian. The word refers to savory flans or soufflés (in this case, a chilled aspic) served as a *primo*, or first course. When made well, they are a direct expression of the main ingredient itself. We use medium-size red heirloom tomatoes for this recipe. It works well with either red or yellow varieties. The most important thing is that the tomatoes be ripe, juicy, and delicious. Use a flavorful, high-quality domestic or imported extra-virgin olive oil for drizzling. —Chef Craig Stoll, Delfina restaurant

3 garlic cloves

3 pounds ripe heirloom tomatoes, peeled and seeded (see page 28), juice reserved

1 tablespoon red wine vinegar

Pinch of red pepper flakes

Kosher salt to taste

4 teaspoons unflavored gelatin

2 tablespoons chopped fresh basil

Extra-virgin olive oil for drizzling

Freshly ground black pepper to taste

Wine Pairing: Chardonnay

Mash the garlic cloves to a paste with the flat side of a chef's knife.

In a blender or food processor, purée the tomatoes and reserved juice with the garlic, vinegar, and red pepper flakes (you may need to do this in batches). Strain through a fine-mesh sieve lined with a single layer of cheesecloth. Season with salt. You should have about 4 cups liquid.

Transfer the tomato purée to a medium nonreactive saucepan and sprinkle the gelatin on top. Let stand until the gelatin no longer looks dry, about 5 minutes. Place over low heat, stirring gently, until the gelatin dissolves, about 1 minute. Do not boil. Remove from the heat and let cool for 10 minutes, then stir in the basil. Pour into six 6-ounce glass or ceramic ramekins. Refrigerate for at least 6 hours or overnight to set.

To serve, run a thin paring knife around the inside edge of the ramekins and unmold the *sformatini* onto salad plates. Drizzle with olive oil and sprinkle with black pepper. *Serves 6*

FRIED GREEN TOMATOES WITH ARUGULA PESTO AND CHERRY TOMATO RELISH

● ● ●

Fried green tomatoes are a delicious way to use up unripe tomatoes at the end of the growing season. —Chef John Toulze, The Girl and the Fig

Arugula Pesto

1 tablespoon pine nuts

1 tablespoon walnuts

1 small garlic clove, minced

1/2 cup extra-virgin olive oil

1/2 cup packed arugula

1 teaspoon fresh lemon juice

1/4 cup grated Vella dry Jack cheese or Parmesan cheese

Salt and freshly ground pepper to taste

Cherry Tomato Relish

2 pints heirloom cherry tomatoes

1 tablespoon extra-virgin olive oil

1 tablespoon balsamic vinegar

1 garlic clove, minced

1 teaspoon salt

1/2 teaspoon freshly ground pepper

6 unripe green heirloom tomatoes

3/4 cup buttermilk

1 cup panko (Japanese breadcrumbs)

1/2 cup cornmeal

1/2 cup all-purpose flour

1/2 cup grated Vella dry Jack cheese or Parmesan cheese

1 1/2 teaspoons chipotle powder

1 1/2 teaspoons sweet paprika

1 teaspoon salt, plus more to taste

1 teaspoon freshly ground pepper, plus more to taste

4 cups canola oil for frying

Wine Pairing: Syrah

To make the arugula pesto: In a food processor, grind the pine nuts and walnuts to a fine powder. Add the garlic, olive oil, arugula, lemon juice, and cheese and purée until blended. Season with salt and pepper.

To make the cherry tomato relish: Cut the cherry tomatoes in half. In a large bowl, whisk the olive oil, balsamic vinegar, garlic, salt, and pepper together. Add the cherry tomatoes and mix gently to coat.

Slice off the ends of the green tomatoes and cut each tomato into three 1/2-inch-thick crosswise slices. Pour the buttermilk into a shallow bowl. In a second shallow bowl, mix the panko, cornmeal, flour, cheese, chipotle powder, paprika, the 1 teaspoon salt, and the 1 teaspoon pepper together. Dip the tomato slices into the buttermilk, then into the panko mixture, patting the mixture onto the tomato slices to make sure it adheres.

In a deep, heavy sauté pan, heat the canola oil to 350°F. Add the green tomatoes and fry until golden brown, about 1 minute per side. Using a slotted spatula, transfer to paper towels to drain. Season with salt and pepper.

To serve, place 3 tomato slices and a spoonful of relish on each of 6 salad plates and drizzle with 2 tablespoons of the pesto. *Serves 6*

SWEET AND SOUR GREEN TOMATO TATIN
WITH GOAT CHEESE FONDANT

● ● ●

Warm tomatoes and goat cheese are classically paired here with a tender-leaved, simply dressed spinach salad. The combination of warm and cool, crisp and meltingly soft mixes up a memorable dish full of tastes and textures. With a bowl of soup, this salad would complete a light lunch, or it could start a vegetarian pasta dinner. —Chef Adrian Hoffman, One Market Restaurant

¼ cup sugar

4 unripe green heirloom tomatoes, halved crosswise

½ cup Champagne vinegar

4 unpeeled garlic cloves

½ cup heavy cream, whipped to stiff peaks

4 ounces fresh goat cheese at room temperature

Kosher salt and freshly ground white pepper to taste

Four ½-inch-thick slices levain bread

¼ cup extra-virgin olive oil, plus 1 tablespoon,
plus more for drizzling

6 cups baby spinach

1 teaspoon fresh lemon juice

Wine Pairing: Sauvignon Blanc

Preheat the oven to 300°F. Place a heavy nonreactive ovenproof sauté pan over medium heat and sprinkle in the sugar. Cook until the sugar has melted and is a light caramel color, 3 to 4 minutes. Remove from the heat and carefully add the tomatoes, cut side down. (Caramel is extremely hot, so be careful not to touch it.) Gradually add the Champagne vinegar. Return the pan to medium heat, add the garlic cloves, and simmer until the caramel has dissolved. Place the pan in the oven and cook until the tomatoes are soft, about 30 minutes.

In a medium bowl, fold the whipped cream into the goat cheese with a rubber spatula. Season with salt and white pepper.

Brush the levain slices with the ¼ cup olive oil and season with salt and pepper. Grill the bread over a wood or charcoal fire, or in a very hot grill pan, turning once, until nicely browned, about 5 minutes.

In large bowl, toss the spinach with the 1 tablespoon olive oil and the lemon juice. Place a small mound of spinach on each of 4 salad plates. With two warm spoons, form an egg-shaped *quenelle* of the goat cheese mixture and place on the spinach. Place 1 garlic clove and 2 tomato halves, cut side up, next to the spinach. Spoon 2 teaspoons caramel around the tomato halves, drizzle with olive oil, and place 1 slice of grilled bread on each plate. *Serves 4*

Heirloom Tomatoes Stuffed with Spinach, Artichokes, and Cheese

● ● ●

The simple, quick preparation of this dish belies its depth of flavor and the perfect marriage of its ingredients. Zapotec heirloom tomatoes, with their deeply ribbed sides, would provide elegantly shaped vessels. Alternatively, Persimmon tomatoes, with their bold deep-orange color, would contrast with the green of the spinach. Regardless of the tomatoes chosen, serve this recipe as a side dish or a vegetarian entrée. —Chef Cynthia Callahan, Bellwether Farms

8 large heirloom tomatoes

Salt for sprinkling, plus more to taste

1 pound spinach, stemmed and washed but not dried

1 can (14 ounces) artichoke hearts, drained and chopped

⅔ cup (7½ ounces) crème fraîche, preferably Bellwether Farms

2 cups (8 ounces) shredded Bellwether Farms Carmody cheese or Monterey Jack cheese

2 garlic cloves, minced

Freshly ground pepper to taste

2 cups fresh breadcrumbs

Wine Pairing: Chardonnay

Preheat the oven to 425°F. Cut a ¾-inch slice from the stem end of each tomato and scoop out the pulp and seeds with a soup spoon. (Save the pulp for soup or stock, if you wish.) Lightly sprinkle the insides with salt and invert on paper towels or on a wire rack set on a plate for 20 to 30 minutes.

Put the spinach in a large saucepan. Cover and cook over medium heat until wilted, about 2 minutes. Drain the spinach in a colander until cool to the touch. Squeeze the spinach well to remove as much moisture as possible, then chop finely.

In a medium bowl, mix the artichokes, spinach, crème fraîche, cheese, and garlic together. Season with salt and pepper to taste. Stuff the tomatoes with the artichoke mixture and sprinkle the tops with the breadcrumbs. Place in an oiled baking dish and bake until the filling is bubbly and the breadcrumbs are lightly browned, about 20 minutes. If the breadcrumbs are browning too fast, cover the tomatoes with a piece of aluminum foil. Remove from the oven and serve hot. *Serves 8*

SLICED HEIRLOOM TOMATOES WITH WHITE BEANS AND FRIED OKRA

● ● ●

Okra has a Southern heritage and isn't as well known as it should be elsewhere in the States. You couldn't have a better introduction to it than this dish, with the sweet little pods sliced into rounds and fried to a crunchy deliciousness to contrast with the silky texture of the heirloom tomatoes. —Chef Colleen McGlynn, DaVero Olive Oil

White Beans

1 cup dried navy or cannellini beans, rinsed and soaked overnight in cold water

1 small onion, peeled and cut into quarters

1 carrot, peeled and cut into 1-inch pieces

1 celery stalk, cut into 2-inch pieces

1 bay leaf

1 thyme sprig

Salt to taste

1½ pounds heirloom tomatoes, or a mixture of tomatoes in various colors and sizes, cored and sliced crosswise

¼ cup fresh basil leaves, torn

2 tablespoons DaVero extra-virgin olive oil

2 teaspoons balsamic vinegar

Kosher salt and freshly ground pepper to taste

1 pound young, firm okra

Salt for sprinkling

1 cup buttermilk

½ cup cornmeal

1 cup olive oil or bacon fat

Wine Pairing: Pinot Noir

To make the beans: Drain the beans and combine in a large pot with the onion, carrot, celery, bay leaf, and thyme. Add water to cover by at least 1 inch. Bring to a boil over medium-high heat, reduce the heat to medium-low, and simmer until the beans are tender, about 1 hour. Add more water if necessary so that beans are always covered with liquid. Remove from the heat, season with salt, and let cool in the cooking liquid.

Arrange the tomatoes on 4 salad plates. Scatter the basil leaves over the tomatoes. Drizzle with the extra-virgin olive oil and balsamic vinegar, and season with salt and pepper. Drain the beans, then taste them and adjust the seasoning. Spoon the beans over the tomatoes.

Cut off the stem and tip ends of the okra and slice crosswise about ½ inch thick. Put the okra in a colander, sprinkle with salt, and let drain for about 5 minutes. Transfer the okra to a bowl and add the buttermilk, stirring to coat the okra pieces well. Put the cornmeal in another bowl, drain the okra in a colander, and toss with the cornmeal, shaking off the excess.

In a large, heavy sauté pan, heat the oil or bacon fat over medium heat. Add the okra and fry, stirring occasionally, until nicely browned, about 5 minutes Using a slotted spoon, transfer to paper towels to drain.

To serve, salt the okra lightly and scatter over the tomatoes. Serve at once. *Serves 4*

SAVORY HEIRLOOM TOMATO BREAD PUDDING

● ● ●

In this dish, the simple ingredients of bread, wine, tomatoes, and cheese suddenly, miraculously, become a lighter-than-air soufflé, without separating eggs and beating whites. Raisins and Zinfandel add a fruity complement to the tomatoes and cheese. Try serving this dish as the perfect accompaniment to grilled or roasted meats. —Kendall-Jackson Culinary Team

2 pounds red heirloom tomatoes, peeled, seeded (see page 28), and diced

¼ cup white Zinfandel wine

¼ cup raisins

3 tablespoons chopped fresh basil leaves

3 tablespoons packed brown sugar

1 teaspoon Worcestershire sauce

Pinch of cayenne pepper

1 loaf (1 pound) day-old bread, crust on, cut into 1-inch cubes

4 tablespoons unsalted butter, melted

1 cup (4 ounces) shredded Monterey Jack cheese

Wine Pairing: Riesling

Preheat the oven to 400°F. Grease an 8-by-12-inch baking dish, or one of similar size.

In a small saucepan, combine the tomatoes, wine, raisins, basil, brown sugar, Worcestershire sauce, and cayenne. Simmer over medium-low heat, stirring occasionally, for 10 minutes. In a large bowl, toss the bread cubes with the butter and cheese, then add the tomato mixture and toss again. Spread the mixture in the prepared baking dish in an even layer and bake until nicely browned, 25 to 30 minutes.

To serve, cut into 6 pieces and serve warm on warmed plates. *Serves 6*

MAIN COURSES

BAKED STUFFED HEIRLOOM TOMATOES WITH LOBSTER SAUCE

● ● ●

Pairing heirloom tomatoes with succulent chunks of lobster raises these incomparable beauties to new heights.
Choose large beefsteak tomatoes like Georgia Streak to hold the generous portions of lobster. —Chef Michael Dunn, Yankee Pier restaurant

1 teaspoon extra-virgin olive oil

½ cup finely chopped onion

2 garlic cloves, minced

6 tablespoons unsalted butter

12 Ritz crackers, crushed

1 tablespoon minced fresh flat-leaf parsley

1 teaspoon minced fresh thyme

1 tablespoon fresh lemon juice

1¼ cups coarsely chopped cooked lobster

Kosher salt and freshly ground pepper to taste

3 large heirloom beefsteak tomatoes, about 1 pound each

Lobster Sauce

1½ cups lobster or shellfish stock (available frozen in
      some fish stores and gourmet markets)

2 tablespoons heavy cream

1½ teaspoons brandy

8 tablespoons unsalted butter

¼ cup cooked lobster meat

Kosher salt and freshly ground pepper to taste

Wine Pairing: Chardonnay

Preheat the oven to 350°F. In a large sauté pan, heat the olive oil over medium heat and sauté the onion until translucent, about 5 minutes. Add the garlic and sauté for 3 minutes. Add the butter and simmer for 5 minutes. Do not let the onion brown. Remove from the heat and add the cracker crumbs, stirring to coat them with butter. Add the parsley, thyme, and lemon juice. Set aside and let cool.

Add the 1¼ cups lobster meat to the crumb mixture and stir well. Season with salt and pepper. Cut the tomatoes in half and trim the ends so they sit flat. Scoop out the tomato pulp to form a cup. Salt and pepper the tomatoes and fill with the lobster mixture. Place the tomatoes in a baking dish and bake until the lobster mixture is heated through, about 10 minutes. Be careful not to overcook the tomatoes.

To make the lobster sauce: In a small saucepan, simmer the stock until reduced to ½ cup. Add the heavy cream and simmer until sauce starts to thicken. Add the brandy. Turn off the heat and whisk in the butter, a tablespoon at a time, waiting until each tablespoon is melted before adding the next. Fold in the ¼ cup lobster meat. Season with salt and pepper.

To serve, place a stuffed tomato half on each of 6 plates and spoon 2 tablespoons of lobster sauce over each serving. *Serves 6*

Ricotta Gnocchi with Heirloom Tomatoes and Basil

● ● ◉

A mixture of heirloom tomatoes, such as Brandywine, Morrel, and Green Zebra, creates the tastiest and most visually attractive dish. This is a fast and fresh tomato sauce that shows off the flavor and natural integrity of the heirlooms. —Chef Justine Miner, RNM restaurant

Ricotta Gnocchi

1 pound fresh whole-milk ricotta cheese

2 egg yolks

¾ cup all-purpose flour, plus more as needed

½ cup (2 ounces) grated Parmesan cheese

1 teaspoon kosher salt

¼ teaspoon freshly ground pepper

1 tablespoon unsalted butter

3 tablespoons extra-virgin olive oil

3 garlic cloves, minced

2 or 3 large heirloom tomatoes, cut into ½-inch dice

¼ cup julienned fresh basil leaves

Kosher salt and freshly ground pepper to taste

¼ cup (1 ounce) grated Parmesan cheese

Wine Pairing: Chardonnay

To make the gnocchi: In a large bowl, combine the ricotta, egg yolks, the ¾ cup flour, Parmesan cheese, salt, and pepper and stir well to make a moist but not sticky dough. Gradually add extra flour if needed, 1 tablespoon at a time, but avoid making the dough too dry. Divide the dough into 4 pieces. With well-floured hands, roll each piece into a ¾-inch rope on a floured work surface. Cut each rope into 1-inch pieces and place on a parchment-lined baking sheet that has been heavily dusted with flour. Cover with a dry kitchen towel and use the same day, or freeze on the baking sheet, then transfer to plastic bags to freeze for up to 2 months.

In a large nonstick, nonreactive sauté pan, melt the butter with 2 tablespoons of the olive oil over medium heat until the butter is foaming but not brown. Add the gnocchi, dusting off the excess flour first. Sauté the gnocchi over medium heat, turning carefully with a spatula, until golden brown on all sides and cooked through, about 5 minutes total.

Add the garlic to the pan and cook for 1 minute, being careful not to let the garlic brown. Add the tomatoes and basil and toss with the gnocchi for a minute or two just until the tomatoes are heated through. Do not overcook them. Add the remaining 1 tablespoon olive oil and season with salt and pepper.

To serve, divide the gnocchi among 4 warmed shallow bowls and sprinkle with the ¼ cup Parmesan. *Serves 4*

PACIFIC BAY SHRIMP AND HEIRLOOM TOMATO TARTINE

• • •

Like Italian bruschetta, these individual tartines are topped with a chopped heirloom tomato salad. The additional topping of bay shrimp in a saffron aioli makes the tartines a wonderful light lunch when served with a small green side salad. —Chef Liz Ozanich, Seafood Brasserie

8 ounces bay (cocktail) shrimp

1/2 cup Saffron Aioli (recipe follows)

4 thick slices levain olive bread, preferably from
    Artisan Bakery

4 tablespoons extra-virgin olive oil, such as DaVero

1 cup mixed heirloom cherry tomatoes, halved

1 pound assorted large heirloom tomatoes, such as
    Lemon Boy and Marvel Stripe, cut into 1/2-inch dice

1 small red onion, thinly sliced

2 tablespoons mixed minced fresh herbs, such as basil,
    flat-leaf parsley, chives, chervil, and/or thyme

4 teaspoons sherry vinegar

Kosher salt and freshly ground pepper to taste

Wine Pairing: Chardonnay

In a medium bowl, toss the bay shrimp in the aioli to coat well. Cover and refrigerate.

Preheat the oven to 400°F. Drizzle the bread slices with 2 tablespoons of the olive oil, place on a baking sheet, and bake until nicely browned, about 15 minutes. In a large bowl, combine the tomatoes, onion, herbs, the remaining 2 tablespoons olive oil, and vinegar. Toss gently to combine. Season with salt and pepper.

To serve, place a slice of toasted bread on each of 4 salad plates and top with 1/2 cup of the tomato salad. Pile 1/2 cup of the shrimp salad on top of each tomato salad. *Serves 4*

1/4 teaspoon saffron threads

Juice and grated zest of 1 lemon

2 egg yolks

2 garlic cloves, minced, or 1 teaspoon granulated garlic

1/4 teaspoon Dijon mustard

1 cup virgin olive oil

Kosher salt and freshly ground pepper to taste

SAFFRON AIOLI

In a medium bowl, combine the saffron and lemon juice. Let stand for about 10 minutes to infuse the saffron color into the lemon juice. Whisk in the egg yolks, lemon zest, garlic, and mustard. Very gradually, beginning with just a few drops, drizzle the olive oil into the egg yolk mixture while whisking constantly. Season with salt and pepper. Cover and store leftover aioli in the refrigerator for up to 4 days. *Makes about 1 1/2 cups*

SEAFOOD PASTA WITH HEIRLOOM TOMATO FRA DIAVOLO SAUCE

• • •

This deceptively simple seafood pasta delivers a quick weeknight or casual weekend dinner with all the elegance and taste of a dish that has taken hours to prepare. The rich tomato base for the pasta complements the shrimp and scallops and coats the pasta with a divine spicy-sweet richness.
—Kendall-Jackson Culinary Team

4 tablespoons olive oil

6 garlic cloves, crushed

1½ pounds heirloom plum tomatoes, peeled, seeded (see page 28), and chopped, with juice

1½ teaspoons salt

1 teaspoon red pepper flakes

1 pound dried linguine pasta

8 ounces small shrimp, peeled

8 ounces bay scallops

2 tablespoons minced fresh flat-leaf parsley

Wine Pairing: Pinot Noir

In a large nonreactive saucepan, heat 2 tablespoons of the olive oil with the garlic over medium heat. When the garlic starts to sizzle, add the tomatoes, salt, and red pepper flakes and bring to a boil. Reduce the heat to medium-low and simmer for 30 minutes, stirring occasionally.

In a large pot of salted boiling water, cook the pasta until al dente, about 10 minutes; drain.

In a large nonreactive sauté pan, heat the remaining 2 tablespoons olive oil over high heat. Add the shrimp and scallops. Cook, stirring frequently, until the shrimp turn pink, about 2 minutes. (Cook the shrimp and scallops in 2 batches if your pan is too small to hold them in one layer.) Add the shrimp, scallops, and parsley to the tomato mixture. Cook just until the sauce begins to bubble, 3 to 4 minutes.

To serve, divide the pasta among 4 warmed shallow bowls and ladle the sauce over the pasta. *Serves 4*

HEIRLOOM TOMATO LASAGNA WITH
HERBED RICOTTA, BASIL PESTO, AND WALNUT-RICOTTA SAUCE

● ● ●

This recipe for stylish individual lasagnas with summer-ripe tomatoes is sure to become a family favorite. Although there are a number of steps, each one is quite simple, and the preparation goes quickly. —Chef Adrian Hoffman, One Market Restaurant

Pasta

2 cups all-purpose flour

⅓ cup water

4 egg yolks

1 egg

½ teaspoon extra-virgin olive oil

½ teaspoon salt

Herbed Ricotta

1½ cups whole-milk ricotta cheese

1 egg

1 tablespoon minced fresh flat-leaf parsley

1½ teaspoons minced fresh thyme

Kosher salt and freshly ground pepper to taste

Basil Pesto

½ cup extra-virgin olive oil

2 cups loosely packed fresh basil leaves

2 tablespoons pine nuts, toasted (see note)

2 tablespoons grated Parmesan cheese

1 garlic clove, minced

Kosher salt to taste

To make the pasta: In a food processor, combine all the ingredients and process until they form a ball. Knead briefly on a floured work surface. Wrap in plastic and refrigerate for at least 1 hour. Divide the dough into 4 pieces. As you work with a portion of the dough, leave the rest wrapped. Flatten each piece and run it through a pasta machine, progressively making it thinner, up to the second-to-last setting. Cut each piece into three 5-inch squares. Place the pasta squares on a baking sheet that has been dusted with flour and cover with a dry towel.

To make the herbed ricotta: In a medium bowl, whisk the ricotta, egg, parsley, and thyme together. Season with salt and pepper.

To make the basil pesto: In a blender, combine the olive oil, basil, pine nuts, Parmesan, and garlic. Purée until smooth. Season with salt.

To make the walnut-ricotta sauce: In a food processor, combine the ricotta, walnuts, garlic, and salt. Process until smooth. In a medium saucepan, heat the cream over low heat. Gradually whisk in the ricotta mixture and remove from the heat.

To make the garlic breadcrumbs: In a small sauté pan, melt the butter with the olive oil over medium heat. Add the breadcrumbs and stir constantly until lightly browned, about 5 minutes. Add the garlic and sauté until fragrant, about 2 minutes. Stir in the parsley. Spread the breadcrumbs on paper towels to drain.

Walnut-Ricotta Sauce

1½ cups whole-milk ricotta cheese

¼ cup walnuts, toasted (see note)

1 garlic clove, minced

1 teaspoon salt

¼ cup heavy cream

Garlic Breadcrumbs

1 tablespoon unsalted butter

1 tablespoon extra-virgin olive oil

1 cup coarse fresh breadcrumbs

3 garlic cloves, minced

1 tablespoon minced fresh flat-leaf parsley

Fried Basil Leaves

Virgin olive oil for frying

16 large fresh basil leaves

2 tablespoons unsalted butter, softened

1 cup (4 ounces) shredded mozzarella cheese

1 pound ripe heirloom tomatoes, thinly sliced

Wine Pairing: Merlot or Cabernet Sauvignon

To make the fried basil leaves: In a small, heavy saucepan or sauté pan, heat about ½ inch olive oil over medium heat until a basil leaf sizzles when you dip the tip in the oil. Fry the leaves, 4 at a time, until they stop sizzling, about 30 seconds. Using a slotted spoon, transfer to paper towels to drain. The basil leaves will crisp as they cool.

Preheat the oven to 450°F. Butter a large baking dish and the insides of 4 ring molds, each 5 inches in diameter and 1 inch high (see note). Place the ring molds in the baking dish. For each serving, place a pasta square in the bottom of a ring mold, letting the corners come up the sides. Spread the pasta with 1 tablespoon of the basil pesto and sprinkle with 2 tablespoons of the mozzarella. Arrange a layer of the sliced tomatoes on top and cover the tomatoes with 3 tablespoons of the herbed ricotta. Repeat the layers once and top with a third pasta sheet. Sprinkle with 2 tablespoons of the garlic crumbs. Bake for 15 minutes, or until lightly browned. Remove from the oven and let stand for about 2 minutes.

To serve, spoon ¼ cup of the walnut-ricotta sauce onto each of 4 plates. With a spatula, transfer one ring mold to each plate. Run a small knife around the inside of each mold and carefully lift off. Garnish each plate with 4 fried basil leaves. *Serves 4*

Notes: Ring molds can be made from heavy-duty aluminum foil. Fold an 18-inch-long strip of foil in half lengthwise and then fold in thirds lengthwise. Butter one side of the strip with softened butter. Form into a 5-inch-diameter ring with the buttered side inside and staple the overlapping ends.

To toast nuts, spread the nuts on baking sheet or in a pie tin; toast in a preheated 300°F oven until golden, about 10 minutes.

Soft Polenta with Mushrooms, Oven-Roasted Heirloom Tomatoes, Chard, and Sausage

● ● ●

This is the essence of Italian comfort food, satisfying in every way. Long, gentle cooking of heirloom tomatoes caramelizes and concentrates their sugars. Begin cooking the tomatoes early in the day to simplify the preparation time for the recipe. This is a dish to linger over with good friends. —Chef Skip Lott, Montibella Sausage Company

Oven-Roasted Tomatoes

Extra-virgin olive oil for brushing

8 ounces heirloom plum tomatoes, halved lengthwise
    and seeded (see page 28)

Coarse sea salt and freshly ground pepper to taste

Chard and Sausage Sauce

1 pound Swiss chard

12 ounces chicken and sun-dried tomato sausages, such as
    Montibella brand, cut into 1-inch lengths

12 ounces garlic sausage with fire-roasted peppers, such
    as Montibella brand, cut into 1-inch lengths

2 tablespoons extra-virgin olive oil

1 onion, finely chopped

1 small carrot, peeled and finely chopped

5 fresh sage leaves, minced

2 garlic cloves, minced

1 cup dry white wine

2 tablespoons tomato paste

To roast the tomatoes: Preheat the oven to 300°F. Brush a large baking sheet with olive oil and arrange the tomatoes on it in a single layer, cut side up. Sprinkle them with salt and pepper, then turn cut side down. Brush the tops of the tomatoes with olive oil and sprinkle with salt and pepper. Roast the tomatoes until they are dry and shriveled on top but juicy underneath, about 4 hours, reducing the heat if necessary so that they cook slowly without burning. Remove from the oven, let cool on the baking sheet, and cover with plastic wrap.

To make the chard and sausage sauce: Remove the Swiss chard leaves from the ribs, trim and discard the woody bottoms, and cut the ribs into 3/8-inch-wide pieces. Coarsely chop the leaves and set both aside separately.

In a large, heavy nonreactive sauté pan, cook the sausages in the olive oil over medium-low heat, stirring occasionally, until no trace of pink remains, about 15 minutes. With a slotted spoon, transfer the sausages to a bowl, then pour off and discard all but 2 tablespoons of fat from the pan. Over medium heat, sauté the onion and carrot until the onion is translucent, about 6 minutes. Return the sausages to the pan, add the sage and garlic, and sauté for 2 minutes, or until the garlic is fragrant. Add 1/2 cup of the wine and 1 tablespoon of the tomato paste and cook until most of the wine has evaporated.

(continued)

Soft Polenta with Mushrooms

½ ounce dried porcini mushrooms

1 cup hot water

2 tablespoons extra-virgin olive oil

1 small onion, finely chopped

2 garlic cloves, minced

3 cups chicken broth

1 teaspoon sea salt

1 cup polenta

3 tablespoons unsalted butter

¾ cup (3 ounces) freshly grated Parmesan cheese

Freshly ground pepper to taste

Wine Pairing: Cabernet Sauvignon

Cut the oven-roasted tomatoes in half lengthwise and then again cross-wise. Add them to the pan. Add the remaining ½ cup wine, the remaining 1 tablespoon tomato paste, and the Swiss chard ribs. Cover the pan and cook over low heat, stirring occasionally, for 10 minutes. Add the Swiss chard leaves and cook, uncovered, stirring occasionally, until the leaves are tender, about 8 minutes. Remove from the heat and set aside.

To make the soft polenta: Soak the mushrooms in the hot water for 30 minutes. Strain the soaking water through a fine-mesh sieve into a small bowl and reserve. Squeeze the mushrooms dry and chop fine. Set the mushrooms aside.

In a large, heavy saucepan, heat the olive oil over medium heat. Add the onion and garlic and sauté, stirring occasionally, until the onion is translucent, about 5 minutes. Add the chopped mushrooms to the pan and stir for a minute more. Add the chicken broth, reserved mushroom-soaking liquid, and salt and increase the heat to high. When the liquid is simmering, gradually sprinkle the polenta over in a thin stream, whisking constantly until the polenta is incorporated and no lumps remain. Reduce the heat to very low and cook, stirring frequently with a wooden paddle, until the mixture pulls away from the sides of the pan and the grains of polenta have softened, 25 to 30 minutes. Stir in the butter and Parmesan and season with pepper.

To serve, mound some of the polenta onto each of 6 warmed plates. Make a well in the center and spoon the chard and sausages on top. *Serves 6*

SUN-DRIED TOMATO PESTO CHEESECAKE

● ● ●

This savory cheesecake makes a wonderful first course or a light lunch entrée. Its ease in preparation contrasts with the depth of its flavor.
—Pastry Chef Scott Noll, John Ash & Co.

2½ cups panko (Japanese breadcrumbs)

¼ cup chopped fresh sweet basil, plus 5 leaves
        for garnish

¼ cup chopped fresh opal basil, plus 5 leaves
        for garnish

3 garlic cloves, minced

½ cup (1 stick) unsalted butter, melted

Salt and freshly ground pepper to taste

1 cup (8 ounces) cream cheese at room temperature

¾ cup (6 ounces) fromage blanc at room temperature

¾ cup sour cream

½ cup Sun-Dried Tomato Pesto (facing page)

2 tablespoons sugar

2 eggs

10 heirloom cherry tomatoes

Wine Pairing: Pinot Noir

Preheat the oven to 400°F. In a bowl, mix the panko, chopped basils, garlic, and butter together. Season with salt and pepper. Pack the panko mixture into the bottom and sides of an 8½-inch springform pan. Bake until slightly golden, about 15 minutes. Remove from the oven and let cool completely on a wire rack.

Reduce the oven temperature to 325°F. In a heavy-duty electric mixer fitted with the paddle attachment, blend the cream cheese, fromage blanc, and sour cream together on low speed. Add the pesto, sugar, and eggs and blend on low speed for 5 minutes, scraping the sides and bottom of the bowl as needed. Pour the cheese mixture into the crust. Place the cherry tomatoes around the edge of the filling, evenly spaced. Bake until the filling is set and slightly puffed, about 45 minutes. Remove from the oven and let cool completely on a wire rack.

To serve, cut the cheesecake into 10 wedges (use a sharp knife dipped into very hot water, wiping the knife clean after each cut.) Garnish each slice with a basil leaf. *Serves 10*

SUN-DRIED TOMATO PESTO

1¼ cups fruity red wine, such as Gamay or Pinot Noir

1 cup oven-dried heirloom tomatoes (see page 30) or
dry-packed sun-dried tomatoes

1 tablespoon tomato paste

¼ cup pistachios or almonds, toasted and chopped

2 tablespoons roasted garlic (see note)

¼ cup (1 ounce) grated dry Jack or Parmesan cheese

3 tablespoons chopped fresh basil

½ cup extra-virgin olive oil, plus more for storing,
if needed

Salt and freshly ground pepper to taste

In a small nonreactive saucepan, bring the wine to a simmer. Remove from the heat and add the tomatoes. Let stand until plumped and softened, about 1 hour. Drain off and reserve the wine, pressing on the tomatoes lightly with the back of a large spoon to extract the excess liquid.

In a food processor, combine the tomatoes, tomato paste, nuts, garlic, cheese, and basil and pulse until evenly chopped. With the machine running, gradually add the ½ cup olive oil. Thin to a spreadable consistency with the reserved wine. Season with salt and pepper. Use now, or transfer to an airtight container and float a thin layer of olive oil over the sauce; cover, and refrigerate for up to 2 weeks. *Makes 1¼ cups*

Note: To roast garlic, cut a ½-inch slice from the stem ends of 2 heads of garlic. Place the heads on a piece of aluminum foil, cut side up, and drizzle with 1 teaspoon olive oil. Wrap the garlic in the foil so that it is completely enclosed and roast in a preheated 350°F oven until the garlic heads feel soft when squeezed, about 45 minutes. When the garlic is cool enough to handle, squeeze out and reserve the softened cloves. *Makes about 2 tablespoons*

CHEROKEE PURPLE TOMATO BLT WITH APPLE WOOD–SMOKED BACON

● ● ◗

In this version of the BLT, one of the world's most famous sandwiches, Cherokee Purple tomatoes,
with their inherent depth of flavor and sweetness, are paired with smoked bacon, Spanish smoked paprika, and the peppery richness
of arugula and cheese. —Kendall-Jackson Culinary Team

½ cup mayonnaise

1 teaspoon hot pimentón (Spanish smoked paprika)

2 cups baby arugula or mixed greens

1 tablespoon extra-virgin olive oil

8 slices French or sourdough bread, toasted

2 Cherokee Purple heirloom tomatoes, or other large red
    or black heirloom tomatoes, cut into ¼-inch-thick
    crosswise slices

Sea salt to taste

8 ounces apple wood–smoked bacon, such as Hobbs',
    cooked until crisp and drained

4 ounces dry Jack or semi-dry Jack cheese, such as
    Vella Mezzo Secco, shaved or thinly sliced

Wine Pairing: Syrah

In a small bowl, whisk the mayonnaise and pimentón together. In a medium bowl, gently toss the arugula or mixed greens with the olive oil to coat. Spread 1 tablespoon mayonnaise on each slice of toast. Layer 4 of the toast slices with the tomatoes, a pinch of salt, the bacon, cheese, and dressed arugula. Top with the remaining toast slices to make 4 sandwiches.

Serves 4

CRAB CAKES WITH TOMATO-CORN RELISH AND CITRUS AIOLI

● ● ●

Crab cakes accompanied by this tangy-sweet cherry tomato–corn relish make a delicious lunch dish or a first course for a fancy dinner. The aioli and tomato relish can be made ahead of time. —Chef Josh Silvers, Syrah restaurant

12 ounces fresh lump crabmeat, picked over for shells
½ cup mayonnaise
3 tablespoons finely diced red bell pepper
3 tablespoons finely diced celery
2 tablespoons finely diced red onion
1 tablespoon minced fresh flat-leaf parsley
1 tablespoon fresh lemon juice
3 cups panko (Japanese breadcrumbs)
Salt and freshly ground pepper to taste

Citrus Aioli
1 egg yolk
Grated zest and juice of 1 lemon
Grated zest and juice of 1 lime
2 garlic cloves, minced
½ teaspoon salt
1 cup extra-virgin olive oil

Tomato-Corn Relish
3 ears corn, shucked and steamed for 5 minutes
2 pints sweet heirloom cherry tomatoes, halved
¼ cup rice vinegar
2 tablespoons chopped fresh cilantro
Salt and freshly ground pepper to taste

Canola oil for frying

Wine Pairing: Chardonnay

In a large bowl, combine the crabmeat, mayonnaise, bell pepper, celery, onion, parsley, and lemon juice and stir to mix thoroughly. Add 1 cup of the panko and mix well, adding a bit more if needed until the mixture holds together. Season with salt and pepper. Spread the remaining panko in a shallow bowl or pie plate. Form the crabmeat mixture into 6 cakes and dip them into the panko, patting well so that the panko adheres. Place the crab cakes on a parchment-lined baking sheet and refrigerate.

To make the citrus aioli: In a food processor, combine the egg yolk, citrus zests and juices, garlic, and salt and process for 1 minute. With the machine running, gradually add the oil to make an emulsified sauce. Cover and refrigerate until ready to serve.

To make the tomato-corn relish: Using a large, sharp knife, cut the kernels from the corn cobs. In a large bowl, combine the corn kernels, cherry tomatoes, vinegar, and cilantro and toss well. Season with salt and pepper.

In a large sauté pan, heat ½ inch canola oil over medium heat. Fry the crab cakes, turning once, until browned, about 4 minutes on each side. Using a slotted spatula, transfer to paper towels to drain.

Serve on warmed plates, with the aioli and relish on the side. *Serves 6 as a first course, 2 as a main course*

PRESERVES + SWEETS

TOMATO-GINGER CHUTNEY

● ● ●

This tomato chutney is quick and easy to prepare. We like to serve it with crab cakes when Dungeness crab is in season, but it also livens up cream cheese sandwiches and pairs well with cold meats for lunch or a casual dinner. —Chef Jeffrey Reilly, The Duck Club Restaurant

3 pounds heirloom tomatoes, peeled (see page 28), diced, and drained

3 garlic cloves, minced

1½ tablespoons grated ginger

1 teaspoon red pepper flakes

⅓ cup sugar

⅓ cup apple cider vinegar

2 tablespoons minced fresh cilantro

1 teaspoon ground cumin

1 teaspoon kosher salt

In a large nonreactive saucepan, combine the tomatoes, garlic, ginger, and red pepper flakes. Bring to a simmer over medium heat and cook, stirring frequently, until almost dry, about 15 minutes. Stir in the sugar, vinegar, cilantro, cumin, and salt and simmer until thick, about 5 minutes. Remove from the heat and let cool. Pour into 3 sterilized half-pint jars, seal, and refrigerate for up to 1 month. *Makes 3 half-pints*

BLACK PLUM TOMATO MARMALADE

● ● ●

A great accompaniment to cheeses, this marmalade is also excellent on sandwiches or as a component in a savory dish that works well with sweet and sour flavors, such as pork, lamb, or duck. —Chef John Besh, Restaurant August

5 pounds Black Plum tomatoes, peeled, seeded
    (see page 28), and diced

1½ cups sherry vinegar

1 cup sugar

Grated zest and juice of 1 orange

Grated zest and juice of 1 lemon

10 peppercorns, tied in a small piece of cheesecloth

½ teaspoon cumin seeds

3 jalapeño chilies, seeded and minced

¼ teaspoon sea salt

In a large, heavy nonreactive pot, combine all the ingredients. Bring to a simmer, reduce the heat to medium-low, and cook, stirring occasionally, until thick and jamlike, about 2 hours. Toward the end of the cooking time, place a heat deflector under the pot and stir more frequently to prevent the marmalade from scorching. Remove the peppercorns.

While still hot, ladle the marmalade into 3 hot sterilized half-pint canning jars, leaving ½ inch of headroom. Seal with hot lids and process the jars in a boiling-water bath for 10 minutes, or follow the directions that come with the canning jars. Remove the jars, let cool, and store in a cool, dark place for up to 1 year. Or, if you do not wish to can the marmalade, skip the boiling-water bath and store the jars in the refrigerator for up to 1 month. *Makes 3 half-pints*

SMOKED HEIRLOOM TOMATO KETCHUP

● ● ●

Move over, Heinz—once people taste this ketchup, they won't go back to the store-bought variety. A dollop of this ketchup will take grilled hamburgers to new heights and turn French fries into ambrosia. —Chef Jeffrey Madura, John Ash & Co.

5 pounds heirloom plum tomatoes

1 cup chopped onion

¼ cup chopped red bell pepper

¼ cup chopped celery with leaves

1 garlic clove, minced

1 tablespoon salt

1 cup Champagne vinegar

1½ teaspoons mustard seeds

1½ teaspoons allspice berries

½ stick cinnamon, crushed

1½ teaspoons black peppercorns

1 bay leaf

½ teaspoon cloves

1 teaspoon coriander seeds

⅛ teaspoon celery seeds

⅛ teaspoon red pepper flakes

¼ cup packed dark brown sugar

2 tablespoons granulated sugar

Few drops of hot sauce

1 cup tomato paste

To smoke the tomatoes, use a stove-top smoker with apple-wood pellets, or a wok. Be sure to have a good fan or hood unit to keep the smoke out of the house. If using a smoker, heat it over medium heat until the pellets start to smoke, then add the tomatoes. Smoke until the tomatoes are slightly softened and the skins start to split, 10 to 15 minutes. If using a wok, place 1 cup pellets in the bottom of the wok and place over high heat. When the pellets start to smoke, place a layer of tomatoes on a wire rack about 2 inches above the pellets and cover the wok tightly with aluminum foil, then with the lid. If necessary, add more pellets to smoke the remaining tomatoes.

Quarter the smoked tomatoes and put them in a large nonreactive pot. Bring to a boil over medium-high heat. Cook, stirring frequently, until the tomatoes fall apart, about 30 minutes. Add the onion, bell pepper, celery, garlic, salt, and vinegar. Bring to a boil.

Tie the seeds, herbs, spices, and red pepper flakes in a cheesecloth square or enclose in a large tea ball. Add to the pot with the brown sugar, granulated sugar, and hot sauce. Cook over medium-high heat, stirring often, until the ketchup thickens, 30 to 45 minutes. Remove the spices and purée the tomato mixture using a food mill or a food processor. Discard the pulp and strain the tomato mixture through a medium-mesh sieve. Stir in the tomato paste.

If the ketchup is not thick enough, return it to the pot and boil slowly, stirring constantly to prevent burning, until it mounds up slightly in a spoon. (The ketchup will thicken more when completely cooled.) Taste and adjust the seasoning. Use the same day, or cover and refrigerate for up to 1 month. Reheat to serve. *Makes 5 cups*

HEIRLOOM TOMATO SORBET

● ● ●

Serve this sorbet on a hot summer day, and suddenly the temperature will seem to drop under its influence. Once you have tried the master recipe, you will want to experiment with variations. Try tomato basil, tomato orange or lime, and tomato jalapeño. —Chef Anthony Bonviso, Fiorello's Artisan Gelato

2 pounds full-flavored heirloom tomatoes, peeled and seeded (see page 28)

1 cup water

¾ cup sugar

1 teaspoon salt

2 tablespoons distilled white vinegar

½ teaspoon freshly ground pepper

¼ cup Cabernet Sauvignon wine (optional)

In a blender, purée the tomatoes until smooth. Strain through a fine-mesh sieve.

In a nonreactive saucepan, combine the water, sugar, and salt. Stir over medium heat until the sugar is dissolved. Stir in the tomato purée, vinegar, pepper, and wine, if using. Freeze in an ice cream maker according to the manufacturer's directions. *Makes 1 quart*

ROASTED CHERRY TOMATO AND CINNAMON-BASIL ICE CREAM

● ● ◉

For this ultimate savory-sweet treat, it's important to select the most flavorful cherry tomatoes. The amount of sunshine in each little red fruit cherry will indicate how much punch your ice cream will deliver. Hopefully, you have a local produce person who can tell you when the tomatoes were picked—preferably the same day! —Chef Laura Howard, Laloo's Goat's Milk Ice Cream Company

1 pint heirloom cherry tomatoes

Kosher salt for sprinkling

2 cups heavy cream

1 1/2 cups goat's milk

1/2 cup torn fresh cinnamon basil leaves,
   or 1/2 cup torn sweet basil leaves plus
   1 cinnamon stick, crushed

5 egg yolks

2/3 cup sugar

1 teaspoon vanilla extract

Preheat the oven to 400°F. Arrange the cherry tomatoes, cut side up, on a baking sheet in a single layer and sprinkle with the kosher salt. Roast for about 30 minutes, or until slightly wrinkled. Remove from the oven and let cool.

In a medium saucepan over medium heat, heat the cream, goat's milk, and basil, stirring occasionally, until bubbles form around the edges of the pan. In a large bowl, whisk the egg yolks, sugar, and vanilla together. Gradually pour the cream mixture into the egg yolk mixture, whisking constantly. Pour this mixture back into the saucepan. Wash the bowl and set a fine-mesh sieve over it.

Place the saucepan back over low heat and cook, stirring constantly, with a wooden spoon, until the mixture coats the back of the spoon, or until it registers 165°F on a thermometer. Immediately strain the mixture into the bowl. Discard the basil and push on the cherry tomatoes with the back of a large spoon to extract all the juices. Set the bowl into a larger bowl of ice and stir occasionally until cool. Cover and refrigerate for at least 2 hours to chill.

Transfer the mixture to an ice cream maker and freeze according to the manufacturer's instructions. *Makes 1 1/2 quarts; serves 6*

Left to right: Heirloom Tomato Sorbet (page 105); Roasted Cherry Tomato and Cinnamon-Basil Ice Cream (this page)

TOMATO, GOAT CHEESE, AND LEMON-BASIL CUSTARD WITH A BLACK PEPPER CRUST

● ● ●

This savory crème brûlée combines the surprising taste of a crunchy-sweet caramelized crust with the tang of freshly ground black pepper and ripe heirloom tomatoes. —Chef Jeffrey Madura, John Ash & Co.

1 pound full-flavored heirloom tomatoes, peeled and
    seeded (see page 28)

4 cups heavy cream

1 teaspoon kosher salt

10 egg yolks

¾ cup sugar, plus ½ cup

6 ounces fresh goat cheese, crumbled

¼ cup chopped fresh lemon basil, or sweet basil plus
    1 teaspoon grated lemon zest

8 heirloom cherry tomatoes in various colors

1 teaspoon freshly ground pepper

Preheat the oven to 300°F. In a blender, purée the tomatoes until smooth. Strain through a sieve.

In a medium saucepan, heat the cream and salt until bubbles form around the edges of the pan. In a medium bowl, whisk the egg yolks and the ¾ cup sugar together until blended. Gradually whisk in the hot cream until blended. Strain the mixture into a pitcher or a bowl with a pour spout and skim off any bubbles. Gently stir in the tomato purée, goat cheese, and lemon basil until the goat cheese is melted.

Divide the mixture among eight ¾-cup ramekins placed in a roasting pan. Drop 1 cherry tomato into each ramekin. Fill the pan with boiling water to reach halfway up the sides of the ramekins. Cover loosely with aluminum foil and bake until the centers of the custards are just beginning to set and are no longer liquid, 55 to 65 minutes.

Remove the ramekins from the roasting pan and let cool completely. Cover and refrigerate for at least 5 hours or overnight.

Just before serving, combine the ½ cup sugar and the pepper in a small bowl. Preheat the broiler and sprinkle 1 tablespoon of the sugar mixture evenly over the top of each custard. Broil 2 inches from the heat source just until the sugar is caramelized, about 5 minutes. Let cool for a few minutes and serve warm. *Serves 8*

TOMATO SHORTCAKES WITH
STAR ANISE SYRUP AND CRÈME FRAÎCHE

• • •

Here is a dessert to get your guests talking. The shortcakes are easy to prepare, and the scrumptious cherry tomato filling quite surprisingly delicious. After a few tentative bites, the plates will be quickly emptied. —Chef Carrie Brown, Jimtown Store

Shortcakes

¾ cup unbleached all-purpose flour

¼ cup fine yellow cornmeal, preferably stone-ground

1 tablespoon sugar

1½ teaspoons baking powder

½ teaspoon baking soda

½ teaspoon salt

2 tablespoons cold unsalted butter, cut into ½-inch pieces

½ cup crème fraîche

Star Anise Syrup

½ cup sugar

½ cup water

1 star anise pod

Filling

1½ pints mixed-color cherry tomatoes

Kosher or sea salt for sprinkling

½ cup crème fraîche

Fennel fronds for garnish

To make the shortcakes: Position a rack in the center of the oven and preheat the oven to 450°F. Sift the flour, cornmeal, sugar, baking powder, baking soda, and salt together into a medium bowl. Add the butter and, using a pastry cutter or two dinner knives, cut it into the flour until the bits are the size of small peas. Add the crème fraîche and stir just until moistened. Gather the dough into a rough ball and gently knead it 5 or 6 times in the bowl until it comes together.

On a lightly floured surface, pat or roll the dough out to a ½-inch thickness. Using a 2½-inch round cutter, cut out 5 biscuits. Gather the scraps into a ball, roll or pat the dough out again, and cut out 1 more biscuit. Transfer the biscuits to a baking sheet. Cover and refrigerate while you make the syrup and filling, or for up to 1 day.

To make the syrup: In a small saucepan, combine all the ingredients and bring to a boil over medium heat. Reduce the heat to low and simmer until the sugar dissolves. Remove from the heat and let cool to room temperature. Remove the anise pod. Use the syrup now, or cover and refrigerate for up to 3 weeks.

To make the filling: Slice the cherry tomatoes in half, or in quarters if large, and put in a bowl. Sprinkle the tomatoes lightly with salt. Toss with the star anise syrup.

Bake the shortcakes for 10 minutes, then reduce the oven temperature to 425°F and bake until golden brown, another 8 to 10 minutes. Transfer to a wire rack to cool. (You may also bake the biscuits in advance and serve them at room temperature.)

To serve, split the shortcakes and place the bottoms on dessert plates. Spoon the tomatoes over the cakes, dividing them equally. Be sure to spoon plenty of syrup over the cakes. Place a generous dollop of crème fraîche on the tomatoes. Place the shortcake tops at a jaunty angle on the crème fraîche and garnish with a fennel frond. *Serves 6*

GROWING + CULTIVATING

Growing tomatoes in your own vegetable garden may seem like a simple way to procure excellent tomatoes close at hand to the cutting board and the sauté pan. However, be forewarned. As the participants in the Kendall-Jackson Heirloom Tomato Festival will attest, the cult of the tomato can become a life-long passion. Over a couple of growing seasons, the weekend gardener may convert to a tomato missionary, imagining small envelopes plump with seeds saved from year to year, kitchen counters lined with tiny new plants in January, and buckets and buckets of delicious harvest later in the summer.

The joy of eating tomatoes leads quickly to the delight of growing them. Unlike fickle orchids or stolid succulents, tomatoes combine an ease of cultivation with the reward of juice-dripping, flavor-rich fruit. Ordinary gardeners may begin their careers easily enough with nursery starts, but experiencing tomatoes like the ones featured at the Kendall-Jackson Heirloom Tomato Festival will redirect their quest from ordinary tomatoes to extraordinary heirlooms.

Gardeners who can't attend the festival can find heirloom seeds and starts in catalogues, farmers' markets, specialty produce stores, and nurseries. The Internet is an invaluable source for plants and seeds; the choices run into the hundreds. Indeed, Kendall-Jackson grows about 180 varieties every year, so you can imagine how your own garden space may become crowded with prodigious quantities of different heirlooms. And the varieties saved in seed banks number in the thousands.

To choose the best types for your garden, take advice from local experts, master gardeners, or nurseries, or check with the customer service division of seed and plant catalogues to discover varieties that will thrive in your climate and soil. Heirlooms can be tetchy about their growing conditions, and the successful gardener plots like a matchmaker to find the right plants for his or her location.

● ● ● Potting Mixes, Soils, and Prepared Ground

A good-quality potting mix for growing tomatoes in containers yields a soil that retains moisture, drains well, and will not become concrete hard later in the summer. Commercial potting mixes have been sterilized, which allows container-bound tomatoes to grow without the risk of infection from soil diseases. Most tomato plants grow well in a 5-gallon container.

Tomatoes grown in the ground need soil rich in organic matter, well composted and well rotted. This kind of soil has a high content of microbial bacteria, the good bacteria that help keep plants healthy and able to fight off the kind of bacteria that attack tomato roots. It is good gardening practice to incorporate plenty of compost into the soil before planting.

For planting in the ground, prepare the soil two to three weeks before your transplants are ready to set out. If the soil is so wet that it falls off the shovel in clumps, you will have to wait for it to dry somewhat or risk compacting the ground, making it rock hard. When the soil is ready for planting, it will fall off the shovel loosely and easily.

When the soil conditions are right, first remove any existing plant material, such as weeds or plants that you no longer want to grow there. Using a shovel, a spade, or a machine such as a rototiller, add 4 inches of compost or other soil amendments and turn the soil over to a depth of 12 to 18 inches. Water the turned soil and allow any undesirable seeds that may be in the ground to sprout, about 2 weeks. When the ground is damp but not soggy, remove the unwanted plant material once again. Using a hoe or shovel, break up any clods and rake the surface smooth for planting.

● ● ● Fertilizers

Tomatoes need less nitrogen than most other plants. A nitrogen-rich soil will cause tomato plants to grow luxuriant foliage and fewer fruits. For successful fruit production, tomatoes need greater quantities of potassium, calcium, and phosphorus in their soil.

When you plant your young tomatoes, whether in the ground or in a container, be sure to add a source of phosphorus, calcium, and potassium to the planting hole, so the nutrients will be right where the roots can absorb them. Look for an organic fertilizer to supply these nutrients, or use a synthetic fertilizer either in liquid form, to be diluted according to the directions on the label, or in pellet form, which works by a time-release method. If you choose to use a synthetic fertilizer, either liquid or solid, make sure you use one with a 5-10-5 combination of nutrients to fulfill the special needs of tomatoes. Fertilize container-grown plants with a diluted low-nitrogen liquid fertilizer every 2 weeks. Fish emulsion is a good all-purpose liquid fertilizer.

● ● ● Growing Seasons

Tomatoes grow, flower, and fruit at different rates according to their variety. Early-season tomatoes set fruit quickly despite cool temperatures, producing those anxiously awaited first tomatoes before summer temperatures rise. But because of the cooler weather, not as much sugar develops in the plant, so early tomatoes may not have the full flavor or the intense sweetness of tomatoes grown at the height of summer. Mid- and late-season tomatoes need warmer day and night temperatures to develop flowers and set fruit.

When you buy your seeds or plants, notice their growing season, whether early, mid, or late. Note as well the number of days from transplanting to fruiting. Seed catalogues always provide this information, and plant tags in nurseries usually note it on the front or back.

Gardeners living in cooler climates must select early-season tomatoes to get any fruit at all during the summer. If you have a short growing season, cherry tomatoes and early-season varieties will reward you. Try some special growing techniques to get a rush on the season (see "Starting Seeds Indoors" below). If you live with long, hot summers, plant early-, mid-, and late-season varieties to ensure a long succession of harvest.

Very early tomatoes produce ripe fruit in 50 to 65 days, mid-season tomatoes take 65 to 80 days, and late-season plants 80 to 110 days or more.

● ● ● Starting from Seeds and Planting in the Garden Bed

Starting your own tomato plants from seeds is easy, and it offers you the advantage of growing heirloom varieties that nurseries do not stock. If you live in a cold climate with a short growing season, starting seeds inside produces vigorous plants ready for transplanting when the ground warms up. Sow seeds indoors about 8 weeks before the last spring frost. In warmer climates, tomato seeds can be sown directly in the ground later, after the late spring's warmth has brought the ground temperature up to a level that encourages germination.

● ● ● Starting Seeds Indoors

Seeds need an environment of between 70° and 85°F to germinate. Plant the seeds about ¼ inch deep, water lightly, and cover with plastic to make sure the seeds do not dry out. Horticultural heat mats placed underneath shallow propagating trays will provide bottom heat to improve germination. Shopping at your local nursery will turn up myriad containers to

start plants in, from plastic six-packs to peat pots that disintegrate when planted in the soil. If reusing clay pots, be sure to sterilize them in a diluted bleach solution first.

Sprouts will pop up in 6 to 8 days. A sunny south window may provide enough light and warmth, or you can use Gro-lights or full-spectrum lights placed 4 to 6 inches above the containers. If your plants lean toward the light source and look skinny and weak, they are not getting enough light.

After the plants have their first true leaves, transplant them into 3- to 4-inch pots and place them in an area with full light and temperatures of 60° to 70°F. The plants should have at least 8 hours of sun a day. Approximately 7 to 10 days before you want to transplant outside, set the plants in a sheltered area outdoors to accustom them to the outside environment during the day. Bring them in or cover them at night to ensure that late frosts don't nip the young and tender plants. Transplant them outdoors into well-worked garden soil. Plant deeply—up to their first true leaves—so the plants can develop a strong root system. Tomato plants sprout roots all along their stems.

If space is limited, determinate varieties are more space efficient, but they fruit all at once, so you can't expect a long season of fruit unless you grow different varieties. Most heirlooms types are indeterminate, continuing to grow and fruit all season long. They need to be planted 20 to 30 inches apart, with 36 to 48 inches between the rows.

● ● ● Mulch

Mulch is one of the gardener's best tools for growing tomatoes successfully. Adding a layer of insulation above the soil keeps the soil temperature constant, seals in moisture, and inhibits weeds. Straw, compost, dried grass clippings, and wood chips are good materials for mulch. Add a 3- to 4-inch layer of mulch around the stem of the young plant once the ground has warmed up in summer. If you add mulch too soon, it will keep the ground from warming, slowing the growth of your tomato plants.

Some gardeners prefer to use sheets of black plastic as mulch around the base of their tomato plants or along a row of plants. This type of mulch has the merit of raising soil temperatures slightly as well as providing weed cover and moisture control. Other growers prefer a red plastic that works just the same as black plastic but also reflects light up to the tomatoes, which is supposed to help them develop faster.

● ● ● Training, Pruning, and Support

You must know whether you are growing determinate or indeterminate tomatoes in order to select the best training techniques to support mature plants heavy with fruit. Plants grown without support will sprawl, leaving the fruit susceptible to rot and to bug, snail, and slug damage.

Determinate tomatoes grow only to a certain height, so pruning them to control size is rarely necessary. Provide low support to keep their fruit off the ground. Indeterminate tomatoes continue to grow throughout the season, so they should be trellised in order to contain their growth and support the trailing stems heavy with ripening tomatoes.

Tomato plants grow with a central stem and horizontal branches that extend from it, and the fruit is borne on sprays that grow off both the stem and branches. From the crotch where the branch joins the stem, another kind of branch, called a sucker, shoots out. Research indicates that pinching off suckers encourages the plant to set fruit sooner. If you want very-early-season fruit, pinch out the growing tip of the sucker above the first set of leaves. You can continue to prune off the suckers to control growth, but later in the season, many gardeners choose to leave suckers on for additional fruit.

Tall and leggy, indeterminate tomatoes need firm staking. The clusters of ripening tomatoes can be too heavy to be carried without breaking branches or resting on the ground. Provide strong supports, such as a 5- to 6-foot trellis, a strong wire cage, or tall sturdy stakes. Commercial hoops are also available. Choose the largest staking devices you can find and make sure to set them in place when the tomato plant is young. Very quickly, it will become impossible to train your growing tomato plants without breaking their long branches.

Some nurseries and catalogues offer cages that flatten for storage after use—a real convenience. Strips of soft cloth or plastic horticulture ribbon are best to tie the plants loosely to stakes, trellises, and hoops.

● ● ● Diseases

Microscopic organisms cause fungal and bacterial diseases in tomatoes through diseased soil. Once the soil is infected with these organisms, it is difficult to grow heirloom tomato varieties. Keeping your plants correctly watered and fertilized will strengthen their resistance to these diseases, but is no guarantee of success.

Verticillium wilt is a soil-borne fungus that has no cure. Your plants will suddenly begin to wilt at the tips, not recovering even after watering or evening cool.

Fusarium wilt is a soil-borne fungus that manifests as a yellowing of the plant leaves. It starts at the base and moves upward. Like verticillium, it has no cure.

Once you are sure of your diagnosis, remove the plants immediately and dispose of them in the garbage. Do not attempt to compost the vines or you will spread the disease. Dig lots of well-rotted compost into the affected area and don't plant any members of the Solanaceae family, including potatoes, tomatoes, and eggplants, in that location for three years. If you have nowhere else to plant them, grow your heirloom tomatoes in containers with commercial soil mix.

Make sure to rotate the location of your tomato beds or grow succeeding crops in the same location before replanting your tomatoes the next year. Crop rotation helps the soil to recover and is a preventative treatment for soil diseases. Again, layering mulch or compost on top of or digging it into the beds encourages the good microbes that keeps the soil healthy, so make it a garden practice during and after every planting. Empty out containers and mix in new compost and amendments before starting out to replant with tomatoes in the new season.

● ● ● Pests

The most persistent pest for tomato growers is the tomato hornworm moth, *Manduca quinquemaculata*. When fully grown, the 4- to 5-inch green worm looks designed for a science fiction film, but actually it is the caterpillar stage of an enormous moth with a wingspan of up to 4⅜ inches. These hummingbirds of the insect world hover over blossoms at dusk or during the night, drinking their sweet nectar. You can tell that you are housing tomato horn worms when you see frass, their black droppings, on the leaves, or notice that the leaves have been nibbled to ribs, or that the tomatoes have holes eaten out of them. To control the worms, simply pick them off and destroy them. There is no reason to spray an insecticide on your tomato plants.

● ● ● Blossom Drop

Tomato plants will drop their blossoms if night temperatures are too low or too high. Early-season varieties are bred to withstand temperatures of less than 50°F, but most mid-season and late-season varieties will suffer blossom drop if the night temperature falls below 50°F or rises above 75°F . If the temperature is too low, cover the plants with clear plastic or floating row covers: textured fabric that holds in heat and is available from nurseries and catalogues. If you live in areas of high heat, choose the special tomato varieties developed to set blossoms at higher temperatures.

● ● ● The Last Harvest

Inevitably, summer draws to a long golden close, fall beckons with cooler days and chilly nights, and your tomatoes will begin to ripen more slowly. As night temperatures threaten frost, pull up your vines and hang them inside a shed or garage by their roots. Although not all their fruits will ripen, many will continue to ripen, not with the sweetness of full summer, but still tastily. Use some of the unripe green tomatoes in the recipes in this book.

● ● ● Saving Seeds of Heirloom Tomatoes

Joining the throngs of heirloom tomato enthusiasts brings pleasure, whether you are a gardener or just someone who loves to eat tomatoes, but becoming one in a long line of stewards saving seeds and protecting varieties of tomatoes for the future brings a unique pride and joy. Saving your own seeds has a distinct advantage: plants grown for several seasons in the same garden will adapt to that place, improving their ability to flourish in the microclimate and in that specific garden soil.

To start, select tomatoes from the best plants, those that seem the most vigorous and healthy, and pick out the largest, ripest tomato to save. Because each variety has a slightly different genetic code, pick tomatoes from three or more plants of the same variety, if possible. Slice open the fruit and scoop out the seeds in their gel sac into a glass or container labeled with the variety's name. The seeds must go through a fermentation process to destroy seed-borne diseases.

Fill the containers half full with water. Any seeds that float are not viable, so skim them off. Let the containers sit, uncovered, at room temperature until the surface is partially covered with white mold, 3 to 5 days depending on the temperature. Scrape off the white mold and discard, making sure not to remove any of the seeds. Refill the container with clean water and stir. Pour off any floating pulp, again making sure not to discard the seeds. Repeat the process until only the seeds remain in the water. Then, in a fine-mesh sieve, drain the seeds as thoroughly as possible, using a paper towel to wipe the bottom of the sieve dry. Turn the seeds out onto a labeled ceramic, glass, or metal dish, not paper, which would stick determinedly to the seeds when they dry.

Dry the seeds in a warm place out of direct sun, but never at temperatures above 96°F, as the seeds will die at high temperatures. When the seeds are thoroughly dry, store them in glass jars, well labeled with the source of the plant (catalogue, neighbor, nursery, or garage sale), the name of the variety, the date the seeds were collected, and the location. Notes on productivity, neighbors gifted with plants, and any susceptibility to growing conditions are also useful for future harvests. Keeping the seeds dry discourages fungal diseases or conditions that may cause the seeds to sprout prematurely.

● ● ● **Heirloom Tomato Varieties Grown by Kendall-Jackson**

The following is a current list of most of the varieties that Kendall-Jackson grows, although it changes a bit from year to year.

Red/Pink

Abe Lincoln

Amish Red

Andes

Argentina

Arkansas Traveler

Aunt Ginny's Purple

Boxcar Willie

Brandywine

Brandywine Pink

Brandywine Red

Bulgarian Triumph

Chalk's Early Jewel

Chapman

Cosmonaut Volkov Red

Costa Rica

Crnkovic Yugoslavian

D'Australie

Ding Wall Scotty

Druzba

Esikos Botermo

Ethiopia Roi Humbert

Eva's Purple Ball

German Queen

German Red Strawberry

Hungarian Oval

Large Pink Bulgarian

Lida Ukrainian

Marisol Bratha

Marlowe Charleston

Micado Violettor

Oaxacan Pink

Pink Russian 117

Pink Sweet

Porter Improved Pink

Red Georgia

Russian 117

Sainte Lucie

Sandul Moldovan

Shirley Amish Red

Soldacki

Stupice

Tadesse

Ukrainian Heart

Wolford's Wonder

Zapotec Pleated

Zogola

Beefsteak

Andes

Argentina

Aunt Ginny's Purple

Aunt Ruby's German Green

Brandywine OTV

Chapman

Crnkovic Yugoslavian

Dr. Neal

Flammé

Georgia Streak

German Queen

Great White

Limmony

Marisol Bratha

Mortgage Lifter

Persimmon

Sainte Lucie

Soldacki

Zogola

Bicolor

Big White

Georgia Streak

Hess

Marvel Stripe

Northern Lights

Pink Stripe

Tonnelet

Yellow/Orange

Amish Gold

Basinga

Caro Rich

Dixie Golden Giant

Dr. Wyches Yellow

Earl of Edgecomb

Flammé

Golden Grape

Gold Medal Yellow

Hawaiian Pineapple

Iles Yellow Latavian

Jaune Negib

Lillian's Heirloom Yellow

Limmony

Manyel

Orange Queen

Orange Russian 117

Persimmon

Pink Lemon

Roughwood Golden Plum

Stor Gul

Tangella

Yellow Brandywine, Platfoot Strain

Yellow Peach

Yellow Ruffles

White

Great White

Old Ivory Egg

Potato Leaf White

Snow White

Sutton

White Queen

Green

Aunt Ruby's German Green

Emerald Evergreen

Green Zebra

Lime Green Salad

Peppermint

Russian Lime

Black

Black From Tula

Black Krim

Black Plum

Brandywine Black

Brandywine Purple

Carbon

Cherokee Purple

Italian Purple

Paul Robeson

Purple Ball

Purple Price

Cherry/Grape

Aunt Ruby's Yellow Cherry

Blondkopfchen

Crazy

Galinas Cherry

Golden Grape

Grandpa's Minnesota

Green Grape

Mirabell

Peace Vine Cherry

Riesentraube Cherry

Sweetie

Plum

Aher's Plum

Black Plum

Plum Lemon

Roughwood Golden Plum

Paste

Eckert Polish

Eleanor

Martino's Roma

Myona

Pantano Romanesco

Russian Big Roma

RESOURCES

There are dozens and dozens of seed catalogues that sell heirloom tomato plants and seeds. Here are just a few suggestions.

Bountiful Gardens
18001 Shafer Ranch Rd.
Willets, CA 95490
(707) 459-6410
Fax: (707) 459-1925
www.bountifulgardens.org

Cook's Garden
PO Box C5030
Warminster, PA 18974
(800) 457-9703
Fax: (800) 457-9705
www.cooksgarden.com

John Scheepers Kitchen Garden Seeds
23 Tulip Dr.
PO Box 638
Bantam, CT 06750
(860) 567-6086
Fax: (860) 567-5323
www.kitchengardenseeds.com

Laurel's Heirloom Tomato Plants
1725 257th St.
Lomita, CA 90717
(310) 534-8611
Fax: (310) 602-6281
www.heirloomtomatoplants.com

Native Seeds/SEARCH
526 North Fourth Ave.
Tucson, AZ 85705
(520) 622-5561
Fax: (520) 622-5591
www.nativeseeds.org

The Natural Gardening Company
PO Box 750776
Petaluma, CA 94975
(707) 766-9303
Fax: (707) 766-9747
www.naturalgardening.com

Pinetree Garden Seeds
PO Box 300
New Gloucester, ME 04260
(207) 926-3400
Fax: (888) 527-3337
www.superseeds.com

Seeds of Change
1364 Rufina Circle, No. 5
Santa Fe, NM 87501
(505) 438-8080
Fax: (800) 392-2587
www.seedsofchange.com

Seed Savers Exchange
3094 North Winn Rd.
Decorah, IA 52101
(563) 382-5990
Fax: (563) 382-5872
www.seedsavers.org

Southern Exposure Seed Exchange
PO Box 460
Mineral, VA 23117
(540) 894-9480
Fax: (540) 894-9481
www.southernexposure.com

Territorial Seed Company
PO Box 158
Cottage Grove, OR 97424
(800) 626-0866
Fax: (888) 657-3131
www.territorialseed.com

Tomato Growers Supply Company
PO Box 60015
Fort Myers, FL 33906
(888) 478-7333
Fax: (888) 768-3476
www.tomatogrowers.com

Contributors

Artisan Bakers
750 West Napa St.
Sonoma, CA 95476
(707) 939-1765
www.artisanbakers.com

Bellwether Farms
PO Box 299
Valley Ford, CA 94972
(707) 763-0993
www.bellwethercheese.com

DaVero Olive Oil
1195 Westside Rd.
Healdsburg, CA 95448
(707) 431-8000
www.davero.com

Delfina
3621 18th St.
San Francisco, CA 94110
(415) 552-4055
www.delfinasf.com

The Duck Club Restaurant
Bodega Bay Lodge & Spa
103 Highway 1
Bodega Bay, CA 94923
(707) 875-3525
www.woodsidehotels.com/bodega

The Girl & the Fig
110 W. Spain St.
Sonoma, CA 95487
(707) 938-3634
www.thegirlandthefig.com

Gotta Havit Desserts
3100 Kerner Blvd. #HH
San Rafael, CA 94901
(415) 459-8004
www.cal-italia.org

Jimtown Store
6706 State Hwy.
Jimtown, CA 95448
(707) 433-1212
www.jimtown.com

John Ash & Co.
4330 Barnes Rd.
Santa Rosa, CA 95403
(707) 527-7687
www.vintnersinn.com

Kendall-Jackson Wine Center
5007 Fulton Rd.
Fulton, CA 95439
(707) 571-8100
www.kj.com

Laloo's Goat's Milk Ice Cream
3900 Magnolia Ave.
Petaluma, CA 94952
(707) 763-1491
www.goatmilkicecream.com

Langley's on the Green
610 McClelland Dr.
Windsor, CA 95492
(707) 837-7984
www.langleysonthegreen.com

Lark Creek Walnut Creek
1360 Locust St.
Walnut Creek, CA 94596
(925) 256-1234
www.larkcreek.com

Montibella Sausage Co.
PO Box 567
Orinda, CA 94563
(800) 747-1616
www.cal-italia.org

One Market Restaurant
1 Market St.
San Francisco, CA 94105
(415) 777-5577
www.larkcreek.com

Preferred Sonoma Caterers
23 Kentucky St.
Petaluma, CA 94952
(707) 935-7960
www.sonomacaterers.com

Restaurant August
301 Tchoupitoulas St.
New Orleans, LA 70130
(504) 299-9777
www.restaurantaugust.com

RNM Restaurant
598 Haight St.
San Francisco, CA 94117
(415) 551-7900
www.rnmrestaurant.com

Seafood Brasserie
170 Railroad St.
Santa Rosa, CA 95401
(707) 636-7388
www.vineyardcreek.com

Syrah Restaurant
205 Fifth St.
Santa Rosa, CA 95401
(707) 568-4002
www.syrahbistro.com

Yankee Pier
378 Santana Row
San Jose, CA 95128
(408) 244-1244
www.larkcreek.com

Yankee Pier
286 Magnolia Ave.
Larkspur, CA 94939
(415) 924-7676
www.larkcreek.com

Zazu
3535 Guerneville Rd.
Santa Rosa, CA 95401
(707) 523-4814
www.zazurestaurant.com

INDEX

ACKNOWLEDGMENTS

As varied as a platter of heirloom tomatoes, with its visual richness of shapes, colors, sizes, and bursts of tart and sweet tastes, a finished book represents the contributions of many different people.

Kendall-Jackson co-proprietors Jess Jackson and Barbara Banke have hosted and supported the Heirloom Tomato Festival from its inception. Kendall-Jackson vice president of public relations George Rose nurtured the seed for this project, while Chronicle Books editor Bill LeBlond provided a safe haven. Urging the book along were project coordinator Blake Hallanan, design assistant Kristen Wurz, recipe tester Catherine Pantsios, and at Kendall-Jackson, winemaster Randy Ullom, director of hospitality Mark Mathewson, and executive chef Justin Wangler, along with the entire Kendall-Jackson culinary staff. We want especially to thank all the Heirloom Tomato Festival chefs and food artisans who so generously shared their favorite tomato recipes for the book. To capture the visual essence of tomatoes, photographers Dan Mills, Robert Holmes, M. J. Wickham, and Larry Armstrong, food stylist Stephanie Greenleigh, and prop stylist Diane McGauley gathered and sliced, aimed and arranged.

Denise Ward of Passanisi Nursery in Penngrove, California, first developed heirloom tomato mania during a lecture of mine many years ago and has passed her enthusiasm on to hundreds of gardeners. She brought me up to date on all the newly available heirloom varieties. Arann Harris and Paige Green kept the Windrush Farm animals and tomatoes happy while the writing progressed, and Daniel Harris provided continued encouragement. Kendall-Jackson garden director Patricia Rossi and Lou Rex of the Kendall-Jackson Wine Center gave their time and assistance in detailing the history of the festival and tutored me as to the inception of the gardens and the tomato varieties grown there. Carolyn Miller edited the manuscript to smooth away all the ruffled edges. Of course, I am deeply grateful to the insight, skill, partnership, and patience of Jennifer Barry, who first conceived of the project and brought it to fruition.